Formative Classroom Assessment

Formative Classroom Assessment

THEORY INTO PRACTICE

EDITED BY

James H. McMillan

Teachers College
Columbia University
New York and London

Published by Teachers College Press, 1234 Amsterdam Avenue, New York, NY 10027

Library of Congress Cataloging-in-Publication Data

Formative classroom assessment : theory into practice / edited by James H. McMillan.
     p. cm.
   Includes bibliographical references and index.
   ISBN 978-0-8077-4799-5 (pbk. : alk. paper) — ISBN 978-0-8077-4800-8 (cloth : alk. paper)
  1. Educational tests and measurements. 2. Academic achievement—testing. 3. Examinations—Interpretation. I. McMillan, James H.
   LB3051.F65 2007
   371.26—dc22

                                     2007010658

ISBN 978-0-8077-4799-5 (paper)
ISBN 978-0-8077-4800-8 (cloth)

Printed on acid-free paper

Manufactured in the United States of America

14 13 12 11 10 09 08 07   8 7 6 5 4 3 2 1

Contents

CHAPTER 1

Formative Classroom Assessment: The Key to Improving Student Achievement

James H. McMillan

The term *formative assessment* has become a buzzword in education. Sometimes this term means *classroom* formative assessment; other times it may mean something like "using student achievement data to inform instruction" or "benchmark" assessment. The focus of this book is on formative classroom assessment as a set of skills and activities that are undertaken by teachers to provide feedback to students to enhance their motivation and learning by designing instruction to meet student needs (Black & Wiliam, 1998; Chappuis & Stiggins, 2002; McMillan, 2003). Evidence of student learning is used on a daily basis to inform teachers about student progress as learning occurs. Formative assessment provides a structure in which teachers' decisions about next steps (correctives) are based on carefully gathered and interpreted evidence. This process is consistent with cognitive theories of learning and motivation in which active construction of meaning is used to enhance understanding (Brookhart, 1997; Shepard, 2000). Formative assessment helps students see the connections and clarify meaning in small, successive steps as new knowledge is related to existing understandings. Based on comprehensive reviews of studies and subsequent research (Black & Wiliam, 1998; Black & Wiliam, 2005; Brookhart, 2005), we know that the use of effective formative assessment strategies enhances student achievement, whether measured by classroom or large-scale tests.

In contrast, benchmark, or *summative*, assessment is conducted mainly to monitor and record student achievement, and is used for school accountability. The use of such assessment tends to emphasize global rather than individualized learning, and extrinsic motivation. The ultimate goal is high student test scores, accompanied by the assumption that higher test scores mean more student learning (which is incorrect!). Teachers are increasingly pressured to use classroom assessments to prepare students for taking high-stakes tests. Often, this means using multiple-choice tests, which are almost always summative in nature.

If formative classroom assessment is the beauty, then, based on the above and the characteristics summarized in Table 1.1, large-scale accountability testing is the beast. I suppose such labeling is not completely accurate; surely there is some accountability testing that promotes learning, and there is also formative assessment that doesn't promote learning. In an interesting marketing strategy, testing companies recognize the importance of formative assessment, and are now promoting assessment that they call "formative." However, it is more accurate to describe these tests as *benchmark* assessments that provide periodic testing in reading and mathematics that monitors students' progress toward achievement of what is covered on end-of-year high-stakes tests. These tests, which are typically provided by the district or commercial test publishers, are administered on a regular basis to compare student achievement to "benchmarks" that indicate where student performance should be in relation to what is needed to do well on end-of-year high-

Table 1.1. Characteristics of Formative and Summative Classroom Assessment

Characteristic	Formative	Summative
Purpose	Provide ongoing feedback to improve learning	Document student learning at the end of an instructional segment
When Conducted	During instruction	After instruction
Student Involvement	Encouraged	Discouraged
Student Motivation	Intrinsic, mastery-oriented	Extrinsic, performance-oriented
Teacher Role	To provide immediate, specific feedback and instructional correctives	To measure student learning and give grades
Cognitive Levels Emphasized	Deep understanding, application, and reasoning	Knowledge and comprehension
Level of Specificity	Highly specific and individual	General and group-oriented
Structure	Flexible, adaptable	Rigid, highly structured
Assessment Techniques	Informal	Formal
Effect on Learning	Strong, positive, and long-lasting	Weak and fleeting

stakes tests. The reason for the assessments is to gauge student learning, diagnose weaknesses in understanding, and adjust instruction as needed.

Although the term *benchmark* is often used interchangeably with *formative* in the commercial testing market, there are important differences. Benchmark assessments are formal, structured tests that typically do not provide the level of detail needed for appropriate instructional correctives. Such testing tends to interrupt instruction, with minimal meaningful feedback.

The goal of formative assessment is the improvement of student motivation and learning. To reach this goal, teachers must employ a circular, continuing process that involves their evaluations of student work and behavior, feedback to students, and instructional correctives (Figure 1.1). Thus, while teaching, monitoring students, and asking questions, teachers determine what students know, understand, and can do (evaluation), and appropriate specific feedback is provided. This feedback is followed by instructional activities (correctives) that will build on current understandings to broaden and expand learning or correct misunderstandings. New strategies and approaches

Figure 1.1. Formative Assessment Cycle

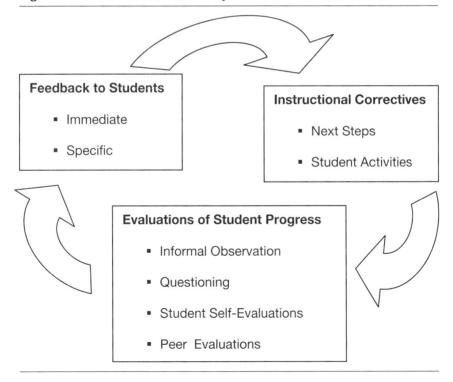

are employed with the understanding that making errors, or being wrong, is a part of learning. Correctives are qualitatively different from initial teaching strategies. Following student engagement with the new learning strategies, additional evaluations of student learning are made, and the cycle is repeated.

To evaluate the efficacy of formative classroom assessment, look for three key ingredients: 1) the extent to which assessments are embedded within instruction; 2) the extent to which additional instructional strategies are employed; and 3) the extent of student engagement and learning.

Of course, external accountability-based testing is a powerful and ubiquitous reality, and it's not going away. Without a compelling alternative, it can do much to make matters worse in schools and classrooms. Because formative classroom assessment is based on established theories of learning and motivation, and has begun to establish a research base, it provides a reasoned and reasonable alternative to drive instruction in much more positive ways. The challenge is to promote formative classroom assessment in a way that stays true to what it should be, to continue research on it to expand the knowledge base, and to identify best practice in implementing it in classrooms.

WHAT'S AHEAD

The intent of this book is to provide context, history, theory, research, and practical application of formative classroom assessment, with the goal of enhancing meaningful student learning. It is structured to provide a balance between theory and research on formative classroom assessment, and practical applications in the context of high-stakes accountability testing and standards-based education.

The chapters are designed to take you from a description of the current context in which formative assessment is embedded, to theory, then to research. The theoretical and research base is used as a foundation for understanding the influence of large-scale testing on the nature of needed empirical studies. The final two chapters illustrate how formative classroom assessment can be applied in the classroom. These examples show how theoretical and research underpinnings are used in specific instructional units.

For the past two decades, the idea that classroom assessment can be used for pupil learning, rather than to monitor what has been learned, has been promoted with enthusiasm by the author of the second chapter, Richard Stiggins. In this chapter, Stiggins identifies the challenges of implementing effective classroom assessment and describes steps for harnessing the considerable power of formative assessment for improving student performance. Stiggins points out that this challenge will only be met when teachers and administrators have adequate professional preparation in the principles of formative assessment.

The second and third chapters frame formative classroom assessment from the point of view of theory and research. In Chapter 3, Dylan Wiliam, perhaps the world's most visible expert on formative assessment, and his colleague provide a theoretical framework for understanding and applying the tenets of formative classroom assessment. They contend that the terms *formative assessment* and *summative assessment* are rooted in the functions they serve. The point is that it is the way assessments are used that distinguishes formative assessment from summative assessment. The framework they present is then illustrated with examples from the classroom. They show how the principles of formative assessment are put into action. Special attention is given to the roles of pupil engagement, proactive regulation, lessons, and feedback loops.

Chapter 4 takes a somewhat different perspective by providing a "state-of-the-art" analysis of formative classroom assessment research. This includes a review and analysis of research on providing feedback to students and the effects of formative assessment on student motivation, building on initial work in this area by the author. Susan Brookhart's theoretical framework for the role of classroom assessment in motivating student effort and achievement provides information that is needed for reviewing studies that pertain to this framework, and for designing research on formative classroom assessment.

Thomas Guskey has written extensively on assessment in the context of learning theory. His chapter shows how the theory of mastery learning is applicable to formative assessment, arguing that the essential principles of formative assessment were identified many years ago in the work of Benjamin Bloom. This resurfacing of mastery learning, with its emphasis on feedback, instructional correctives, enrichment, and instructional alignment, reminds us of Bloom's seminal work and the relevance of that work to today's classrooms. Although most of us think about Bloom in relation to his taxonomy of educational objectives, his ideas about learning and assessment, supported by extensive research, speak directly to what is being accomplished with formative classroom assessment.

Chapters 2 through 5 frame the issues, present relevant theory and research, and begin to show how to implement formative assessment practices in the classroom. The next two chapters take on the beast: high-stakes accountability testing imposed by state and national policies. This movement has had profound effects on schooling, and with the emphasis on assessment for accountability (testing what students know and can do), it has direct consequences for assessment practices in the classroom.

The chapter by Lisa Abrams frames the problem by summarizing the No Child Left Behind Act (NCLB) and other requirements, presenting research on the effects of these initiatives on teachers and students, and delineating how high-stakes testing encourages teaching to the test and shallow student learning. Abrams emphasizes a new and potentially harmful initiative from national testing companies. These companies are now pushing hard for school district business in what they call formative assessment, but what is more accurately called benchmark or small-scale summative assessment.

In the following chapter, Gregory Cizek, a well-known expert on assessment, provides further detail on how large-scale testing policies and procedures militate against the effective use of formative assessment. He shows how the more technical features of large-scale tests, such as subscale score profiles, alignment to standards, bias, and testing accommodations, have implications for the research that needs to be conducted on formative assessment.

The last two chapters focus on the practical classroom application of principles of formative assessment. They show how teachers can apply ideas and tenets summarized in earlier chapters with specific examples to elucidate the process. Chapter 8, by Wynne Harlen, considers formative classroom assessment in teaching science and mathematics. Chapter 9, by Bethan Marshall, targets English, humanities, and social science classrooms. Both of these authors are well established in classroom assessment and have spent years understanding and applying formative assessment principles in everyday classrooms. Topics such as how teachers gather formative information, provide feedback to students, and involve students in formative assessment; peer and self-assessment; student engagement and communication; and barriers to successful implementation are discussed with constant reference to practical application.

CONCLUSIONS

Two recent initiatives speak to the importance of formative classroom assessment, now and in the future. The first is by the Council of Chief State School Officers (CCSSO). It will involve a state collaborative on formative assessment issues, which convened for the first time in October 2006. The collaborative planned a conference in the summer of 2007 on what participants have called a "small-scale assessment." A $1.1 million grant from the William and Flora Hewlett Foundation was awarded in 2005 to the University of Pennsylvania–based Consortium for Policy Research in Education, a coalition of seven of the nation's top research institutions. The focus of this grant is to identify and study tools and approaches that teachers can use as a "cycle of improvement" to decide what students have learned, whether appropriate progress toward learning goals is being made, and what can be done to improve learning.

Both of these initiatives are concerned with formative classroom assessment, and both should provide further research and development on effective formative assessment practices. My hope is that such initiatives use the wisdom of the authors of the chapters in this book to form a basis for continued reflection, research, and practice. Formative assessment is a buzzword. Let's hope that this emphasis translates into meaningful and thoughtful research and applications, including changes in teacher preparation, professional development for teachers and administrators, and the implementation of interventions targeted at improving formative classroom assessment.

REFERENCES

Black, P., & Wiliam, D. (1998). Assessment and classroom learning. *Assessment in Education*, 5(1), 7–74.

Black, P., & Wiliam, D. (2005). Lessons from around the world: How policies, politics and cultures constrain and afford assessment practices. *Curriculum Journal*, 16(2), 249–261.

Brookhart, S. M. (1997). A theoretical framework for the role of classroom assessment in motivating student effort and achievement. *Applied Measurement in Education*, 10(2), 161–180.

Brookhart, S. M. (2005, April). *Research on formative classroom assessment: State-of-the-art*. Paper presented at the meeting of the American Educational Research Association, Montreal, Canada.

Chappuis, S., & Stiggins, R. J. (2002). Classroom assessment for learning. *Educational Leadership*, 60(1), 40–43.

McMillan, J. H. (2003). Understanding and improving teachers' classroom assessment decision making. *Educational Measurement: Issues and Practice*, 22(4), 34–43.

Shepard, L. A. (2000). The role of assessment in a learning culture. *Educational Researcher*, 29(7), 4–14.

CHAPTER 2

Conquering the Formative Assessment Frontier

Richard J. Stiggins

While in third grade, our daughter Kris returned home from school one day with a long face and a single piece of paper in her hand. She immediately apologized to Nancy and me for making us mad. We weren't mad—yet. Then Kris shared the paper—a brief piece she had written. It filled three-quarters of the page (the small "beginning writer" paper with wide lines). We asked her to tell us about it. She recounted that she had been instructed to write about someone or something she loved. As we read, we learned the paper was about Kelly, a little kitten that had joined our family briefly and then had to return to the farm due to Kris's allergies—a very sad day for our family. We had all cried, she wrote (she was right). The writing was pretty good for an emergent writer. The facts were correct, as was a good representation of our emotions. At the bottom of the sheet was a big red "F." When we asked Kris to explain why she received an F, our daughter confessed that the instructions had been to fill the entire page with writing. She had only filled part of her page; therefore, she hadn't followed directions, and so was judged to have "failed."

Without doubt, we had grading issues to address with this teacher. But that's not my point. The point is made by what happened next, which remains as vivid as a movie in my mind all these years later: Our daughter put the paper down on the kitchen table and walked from the room, saying, "I'll never be a good writer anyway." What is critical is the inference she had made about herself based on the assessment results as she interpreted them; what is tragic is that it was an incorrect inference. Her academic confidence was shaken by this incident, which contributed to some pretty important learning issues that we had to address for her during elementary school.

Now fast-forward to her high school English class. The assignment was to read three novels by the same author, develop a thesis statement, and defend it in a term paper referring to the literature. To set pupils up for success, her teacher began by providing the pupils with a sample of an outstanding paper to read and analyze to determine what features made it outstanding. They brainstormed and discussed what made it good in class. Then the teacher gave them a sample paper that was of very poor quality. Again they analyzed and evaluated its features in some detail. Comparing the two papers, they listed essential differences, ultimately collaborating in the development of a set of keys to quality, which they transformed into a set of rating scales that depicted the continuum of quality along each dimension, all in pupil-friendly language and accompanied by examples of pupil work to illustrate each key. Then, with this specific guidance in place, they drafted their own papers. They exchanged drafts, analyzing and evaluating each other's work and providing descriptive feedback on how to improve each. If pupils wanted feedback from their teacher on any particular dimension of quality, they could request it and would receive it. The paper was done when the pupil decided it was done. In the end, not every paper was outstanding, but most were of very high quality, and each pupil was confident of that fact before submitting his or her work for final evaluation and grading. If our daughter's confidence as a writer had not been established by this time, this experience solidified it. She was and still is a pretty good writer both in fact and in her own mind.

What were the essential differences between these two experiences?

- One assessment arose from a highly refined vision of the achievement target, while the other appeared to either have none or was centered on the wrong one.
- One assessment accurately reflected the actual level of achievement of the pupil, while the other did not.
- One wove the assessment process deeply into teaching and learning through productive pupil involvement in quality assessment development and use, while the other did not.
- One resulted in very high levels of pupil motivation and success, while the other yielded the opposite result.
- One was steeped in the principles of effective communication of results by relying on continuous descriptive feedback, while the other relied on the inept use of judgmental feedback.
- One built the confidence of the learner, while the other destroyed it.
- One supported learning, while the other inhibited it.
- One teacher understood the principles of sound classroom assessment practice, while the other obviously did not.
- One served a *formative* purpose, while the other did not.

The principle assessment challenge that we face in schools today is to ensure that sound assessment practices permeate every classroom—that assessments are used to benefit pupils as they did in the second scenario above. This challenge has remained unmet for decades, and the time has come to conquer this final assessment frontier: the effective use of formative assessment to support learning. In this chapter, I will break down this overall challenge into its component parts, analyzing each and describing what we must do to harness the heretofore untapped power of formative assessment as a key school improvement tool. This includes the need to have adequate professional preparation in formative assessment for teachers and school leaders.

THE FINAL UNCONQUERED FRONTIER

Consider accomplishments in the field of educational measurement over the decades. Educators and psychologists have created and refined a wide variety of assessment methods, from selected response formats to more complex and demanding written and performance assessments. Educators have learned much about how to ensure the quality of the scores generated. Not only have educators and psychologists analyzed and refined various conceptual understandings of validity and reliability, but strategies for both estimating and maximizing them have also become increasingly sophisticated. Strategies for scaling test scores have evolved in ways that facilitate various kinds of score interpretation and use in a variety of instructional decision-making contexts. Applications of technology permit test development, scoring, reporting, and information management that can underpin large-scale administration and test use at international, national, state, and local levels with ease and economy. Indeed, measurement processes have worked their way into the communities and neighborhoods of our society and into halls of political power with such force that they are literally driving a nationwide school improvement initiative. Over the past half century and across our multiple levels of testing, society has invested billions in generating accurate evidence of pupil learning at local, state, national, and international levels. Tests represent the very hallmark of quality schools. We have much of which to be justifiably proud.

Yet, behind these considerable accomplishments, there is almost complete neglect of assessment where it exerts the greatest influence on pupils' academic lives: day-to-day in the classroom, where it can be used to help them learn more. Although typical teachers can spend as much as one-quarter to one-third of their available professional time involved in assessment-related activities, almost all do so without the benefit of having learned the principles of sound assessment practice. Until recently, state certification standards failed to reflect an expectation of competence in assessment. Current licensing exams include only the thinnest reflection of this facet of teaching practice. Teacher preparation programs continue to offer little in the way of relevant classroom assessment training. Leadership programs remain almost completely devoid of assessment training, and in-service programs rarely fill the competence gaps created by this state of affairs.

As a result, the issues and challenges we face in using sound assessment practices to encourage and support (not merely to monitor) learning are legion. In this chapter, I will address six of them:

1. Redefining the emotional dynamics of assessment
2. Assuring effective assessment
3. Using assessment *for* pupil learning
4. Effective teacher preparation in formative applications
5. Providing leadership for formative assessment
6. Educating communities, school boards, and legislatures.

This chapter addresses each of these challenges, advocating solutions that will permit us to conquer this final assessment frontier: the productive use of assessment in support of pupil learning.

REDEFINING THE EMOTIONAL DYNAMICS OF ASSESSMENT

Changing schools from places that merely sort pupils based on achievement into places that assure that all pupils will meet standards brings with it the challenge of rethinking the dynamics of assessment. If all pupils are to meet standards, they all must believe that they can. They all must come to believe in themselves as effective learners. This requires the productive use of formative assessment.

As we all look back at our school years, we remember teachers who believed that the way to maximize motivation (and, therefore, learning) was to maximize the anxiety of the learner. The threat of pending summative assessment was the way to do that. The more on edge pupils were, these teachers believed, the harder we would study and the more we would learn. To get more learning, demand it in a louder voice; threaten with consequences of failure; hold pupils accountable for more learning in a summative sense; if a little intimidation doesn't work, use a lot of intimidation. These were familiar emotional dynamics of assessment during our schooling years. Essentially, the role of the layers of local, state, national, and international summative assessments that are so prevalent today is to perpetuate that same constant state of fear.

This belief about the role of assessment fitted nicely into the mission of our schools, which was to rank us from the highest to the lowest achiever by the end of high school—to begin to sort us into the various segments of our larger social system. The amount of time available to learn was fixed, but the amount learned during that time was free to vary: Some students learned a lot, and some learned nothing at all. Able learners built on past success to gain confidence and grow rapidly. On the other hand, pupils who failed to master the early material within the allotted time obviously would fail to master subsequent material. After 13 years of cumulative treatment in this manner, in effect, pupils spread along an achievement continuum that gave rise to rank in class upon graduation.

The emotional dynamics of this process were clear. From the very earliest grades, some pupils rode their own record of success and the corresponding optimism to even more success. From the start, they scored high on assessments and became increasingly confident in school. This confidence gave them the emotional reserves they needed to risk striving for more success because, in their minds, success was virtually assured if they tried. Notice that the trigger for learning success was the pupil's own interpretation of his other assessment results.

But other pupils experienced different dynamics. They scored very low on summative tests right from the beginning, causing them to begin to doubt their own capabilities. They lost confidence, which, in turn, deprived them of the emotional reserves to continue to risk trying. Chronic failure was hard to hide and became devastatingly embarrassing. It became safer not to try. As their motivation waned, so, of course, did their achievement. Notice once again how the learners' own interpretation of their assessment results influenced their lack of confidence and their unwillingness to keep trying.

The important lesson to learn from this retrospective is that each pupil's emotional reactions to his or her assessment results will determine what that pupil thinks, feels, and does in response to those results. Pupils can respond in either of two ways to any set of assessment results, one productive and the other distinctly counterproductive. The productive reaction has pupils seeing the results and saying, "I understand these results. I know what to do next to learn more. I can handle this. I choose to keep trying." When pupils respond in this manner, the assessment becomes productively formative and helpful.

The counterproductive response leaves pupils saying, "I don't know what these results mean for me. I have no idea what to do next. I can't handle this anyway. I quit." When pupils respond this way, the assessment becomes destructive.

Although this latter dynamic was once accepted as part of the ranking process, today it has become very problematic. As a society, over the past decade, we have come to understand that the accelerating technical evolution of our society and increasing ethnic diversity will require all citizens to become lifelong learners. Foundational reading, writing, and math problem-solving proficiencies become essential for all pupils, not just for the "winners." The problem is that we have come to understand that, in the traditional environment described above, pupils in the bottom half of the rank order (plus all those who drop out before being ranked) fail to develop the foundational proficiencies.

As a result, society has asked its educators to raise the bottom of the rank order distribution to a certain level of competence. We call these expectations our "academic achievement standards." Every state has them and, as a matter of public policy, schools are to be held accountable for making sure that *all* pupils meet the standards.

If society wants all pupils to meet standards, then all pupils must start the learning process believing that they can succeed at doing so; they all must be confident enough in their expectation of success to be willing to take the risk of trying. Any other emotional state (such as the state of perpetual fear perpetrated in the schools of our own youth) for any pupil becomes problematic. It is unacceptable to have pupils who have yet to meet standards losing faith in themselves and giving up in hopelessness.

In other words, assessment practices that permitted (and even encouraged) some pupils to give up on learning must be replaced by practices that engender hope and sustained effort for all pupils. In short, the entire emotional environment surrounding the experience of being evaluated must change, especially for perennial low achievers.

The driving emotional force of fear triggered by the prospect of an upcoming test must be replaced by confidence, optimism, and persistence—for all pupils, not just for some. All pupils must believe that they can succeed at learning if they try. They must have continuous access to credible evidence of their own academic success.

Over the decades, both school improvement experts and the measurement community have made the mistake of believing that the adults in the system are the most important assessment users/instructional decision makers; that is, we have believed that, as long as the adults make the appropriate instructional decisions, schools will be effective. To be sure, parents, teachers, school leaders, and policy makers (all adults) make crucial decisions that influence pupil learning, and the more data-based those decisions are, the better. However, this perspective misses the fact that the pupils may be even more important instructional decision makers than are the adults.

Consider, for example, the reality that pupils are constantly deciding if they are capable of learning. They ask, can I understand this stuff or am I just too dense? Is the learning worth the energy I must expend to attain it? Is the learning worth the risk of public failure? If pupils come down on the wrong side of these crucial decisions and thus stop trying, it doesn't matter what the adults around them decide. This is exactly what happened to our daughter in the opening description of her third-grade writing experience. In effect, our pupils have it within their power to render our adult instructional decisions impotent. If a pupil decides that learning is beyond reach for her or him, or that the risk of public failure is too likely, costly, or embarrassing, then there will be no learning, regardless of what we adults decide.

The essential issue for us adults is, what can we do to help pupils answer the above questions in positive productive ways that keep them trying? The good news is that we have solid answers that rely on effective formative assessment and not on intensifying the intimidation. Further, we know what will happen to pupil achievement when we put effective formative assessment practices into operation. I will fill in details about this below when we explore the procedural specifics of using classroom assessment in support of learning. However, the first challenge we face is to embrace a fundamental redefinition of the emotional dynamics of assessment.

ASSURING EFFECTIVE ASSESSMENT

As we confront the formative assessment frontier, a second challenge that needs to be met is to assure the quality of assessments. Over the decades, studies documenting or synthesizing research on the lack of classroom assessment quality abound (see Chapter 4). The challenge that has stymied both the measurement and teacher education communities has been the translation of complex validity and reliability concepts into commonsense terms and strategies that can be taught to, learned by, and applied by teachers as a matter of routine in their classrooms, where the vast majority of formative assessments are used. The key attributes of quality assessments are clear. However, until recently, teacher educators have had difficulty helping novices understand and apply them. Research suggests that four key ingredients can comprise a practical quality-control framework for classroom teachers (Stiggins, Arter, Chappuis, & Chappuis, 2004). If the formative assessment frontier is to be conquered, every classroom teacher must understand and apply these keys to success.

Key to Quality 1: Clear Purpose

The starting place for the creation of a sound assessment is awareness of the purpose of the assessment. If assessment is, at least in part, the process of gathering evidence to inform instructional decisions, then in any specific context, the assessor needs to know:

- What decisions?
- Who's making them?
- What information will be helpful?

The answers will vary profoundly across contexts.

For instance, at the policy level of assessment use, school and community leaders must know if enough pupils are meeting standards. They need once-a-year data on pupil mastery of state standards that are comparable across classrooms and schools to be accountable to the community and to decide how to allocate resources in the service of program success.

At the level of instructional support, information needs are different. Teacher teams, principals, and curriculum personnel need periodic but more frequent evidence to tell them which pupils are meeting which standards so they can bring program resources to bear while there is still time to help those pupils in need.

Finally, day-to-day in the classroom, the key question is, what comes next in learning? The key classroom decision makers are both teachers and their pupils. The assessment information must inform us about where the pupil is now in the progression of learning leading up to mastery of each academic achievement standard, because only then can we know what comes next. Both pupil and teacher must know where the learner is now, how that compares to ultimate learning success, and how to close the gap between the two. Pupils must not wonder *whether* they will succeed, only *when*. Incremental success must always be within reach in their minds. Obviously, teachers and pupils will use continuous day-to-day formative classroom assessments in ways that differ fundamentally from how policy makers and instructional support personnel use their periodic assessments.

Key to Quality 2: Clear Targets

The second key to accurate assessment is the clear, complete, and appropriate articulation of the achievement target(s) to be mastered and assessed. Target definitions begin with state standards. While the learning is unfolding, pupils progress through the levels of proficiency that lead up to each standard. To make this possible, each standard must be deconstructed into a scaffolding that pupils must climb on their journey up to that standard. These continuously unfolding classroom targets (foundations of ultimate competence), then, become the focus of day-to-day formative assessment.

For this deconstruction to be accomplished, each teacher must be a confident competent master of the standards his or her pupils are expected to master. If teachers don't meet this professional standard, then unclear or inappropriate achievement expectations can result, leaving dependable assessment beyond reach. The building blocks of competence that lead up to any particular standard can include the mastery of content knowledge, reasoning proficiencies, performance skills, or product development capabilities. Teachers must be prepared to assess all of these from moment to moment, as learning unfolds for their pupils.

Key to Quality 3: Accurate Assessment

Given the need to provide information to particular assessment users and to assess various kinds of targets in any particular context, each teacher must be prepared to design and build or select quality assessments for each assessment circumstance. This includes the ability to

- select a proper assessment method for the situation;
- build each assessment out of quality ingredients (items, tasks, scoring procedures, etc.);
- include enough items to sample appropriately; and
- anticipate all relevant sources of bias that may distort results in order to minimize them.

Key to Quality 4: Effective Communication

With the information needs of all assessment users identified, achievement expectations in place, and accurate assessments in use, foundations are laid for the implementation of an effective assessment system. Note that all of this prior work is wasted if procedures are not also in place to deliver formative information about candidate achievement into the proper hands in a timely and understandable form.

For communication to work effectively in a formative assessment context, both the assessor and the learner must understand precisely what it is that they need to communicate about—both must agree on the definition of important achievement expectations. Any lack of understanding about what success looks like will serve as a barrier to effective communication and to understanding the true meaning and implications of assessment results. Effective communication also requires the creation of a reservoir of accurate information about each candidate's achievement and the use of symbols that both message senders and receivers understand to mean the same thing.

In formative contexts, one typically relies on the richness of descriptive feedback to inform the learner how to do better the next time. In essence, formative assessment works best when message sender and receiver plan an opportunity to share formative information in a focused environment that is free of distractions. Without this, the connection to improvement may be missed.

If we are to conquer the formative assessment frontier, everyone who will assess pupil learning must understand and apply these keys to quality assessment in all contexts. The vast majority of currently practicing teachers and school leaders have not yet been given the opportunity to learn these things, either in preservice or in-service training.

USING ASSESSMENT *FOR* PUPIL LEARNING

The quality of an assessment is not merely a function of accuracy of the score it yields. We also must evaluate quality in terms of the impact of the score on the learning. This brings us to practical matters of "assessment *for* learning": the use of the formative assessment process and its results as an instructional intervention designed to increase—not merely to monitor and grade —pupil learning. Research evidence gathered in hundreds of studies conducted around the world over the past decade (detailed below) shows that the consistent application of principles of assessment *for* learning can give rise to unprecedented gains in pupil achievement, especially for perennial low achievers. The implications for such gains in raising test scores and closing achievement score gaps are profound.

Perhaps the most unique feature of the assessment *for* learning process is that it acknowledges the critical importance of the instructional decisions made by pupils and their teachers while working as a team—it provides the information they need when they need it. In this context, pupils become consumers of assessment information, too, using evidence of their own progress to understand what comes next for them.

Another unique feature is the treatment of learning targets: Assessment *for* learning requires standards-based curriculum maps to be written in teacher-, pupil- and family-friendly versions so that the trajectory (i.e., what has been learned and what comes next) is clear to everyone throughout the learning process. This leads directly to the second reason why we assess formatively: to build pupils' confidence in themselves and to motivate them to try. Assessment *for* learning enables pupils by helping them watch themselves grow—by entitling them to retain the belief that, if they keep trying, success is within reach for them. The result is productive formative assessment dynamics.

Unlike policy-level or instructional support–level assessment, assessment *for* learning cannot happen just once a year or quarterly or even weekly. It must continue throughout the learning process. To accomplish this, the teacher must play five roles in classroom assessment:

1. To become competent masters themselves of each of the standards their pupils are to master.

2. To understand how those standards transform into the curriculum that forms the scaffolding that pupils will climb on their journey up to each standard.
3. To make classroom-level achievement targets clear to pupils.
4. To transform the classroom targets into high-quality classroom assessments that are capable of accurately reflecting pupil achievement of those targets.
5. To use those assessments over time in collaboration with their pupils to inform key decisions and to help motivate pupils to keep learning.

In practical terms, then, one strategy on which teachers can rely in productive formative assessment is to provide pupils with an understandable vision of the learning target from the beginning of the learning process, along with samples of strong and weak work so learners can see the road to competence laid out before them. This builds confidence among learners by revealing the path to success. Another strategy is to provide pupils with regular access to descriptive (as opposed to evaluative or judgmental) feedback; that is, information that helps pupils understand how to improve the quality of their work. Still another strategy is to engage pupils in repeated self-assessments so they can watch themselves successfully negotiate the road to competence. As pupils watch themselves succeeding, they become increasingly confident. Ultimately, pupils can learn to generate their own descriptive feedback (that is, learn to self-assess) and to set goals for what comes next in their learning. Each of these specific practices draws the learner more deeply into tracking and taking responsibility for her or his own success.

Thus, the pupil's role in assessment environments is to strive to understand what success looks like and to use each assessment to determine how to do better the next time. Assessments become more than one-time events attached to the end of the teaching. They become part of the learning process by keeping pupils posted on their progress and confident enough to continue striving.

RESEARCH ON EFFECTS

When these kinds of formative practices play out as a matter of routine in classrooms, as mentioned previously, evidence gathered around the world consistently reveals effect sizes of one-half to one-and-one-half or more standard deviations, which are directly attributable to the application of effective formative classroom assessment. In his original mastery learning research, Bloom (1984) and his pupils made extensive use of classroom assessment in support of learning in just the same terms as does the assessment *for* learning concept being described here. They reported subsequent gains in pupil test performance of one to two standard deviations (see Chapter 5 for a detailed treatment of this work). Black and Wiliam, in their 1998 watershed research review of more than 250 studies from around the world on the impact of effective assessment *for* learning, report gains of one-half to one full standard deviation, with the largest gains being realized by low achievers. Meisels, Atkins-Burnett, Xue, and Bickel (2003) involved pupils in developing and using formative performance assessments, and reported gains of over one-and-one-half standard deviations on subsequent tests. Finally, Rodriguez (2004) reports effects of similar size in the U.S. Third International Mathematics and Science Study (TIMSS) math performance arising from the effective management of classroom assessment in formative ways. According to these researchers, the expected achievement score gains will rival the implementation of one-on-one tutorial instruction in their impact on pupil achievement, with the largest gains being realized by the lowest achievers, thus reducing achievement gaps.

The key to the challenge of using formative assessment to enhance learning is to find creative ways to help teachers and their pupils tap the power of assessment *for* learning in every classroom. This leads to our next challenge in conquering the final frontier: providing teachers with the opportunity to learn about assessment *for* learning.

EFFECTIVE TEACHER PREPARATION IN FORMATIVE APPLICATIONS

If teachers are to be given the opportunity to learn these things, then undergraduate- and graduate-level teacher preparation programs must begin the professional learning process. Here we confront a problem, the solution to which has evaded us for decades. Assessment training must become a priority in the teacher preparation curriculum. The challenge is for faculties of teacher education schools both to teach and model all of the sound assessment practices outlined above. To be specific, they must assure that the keys to assessment success (as framed above) are satisfied:

- All relevant purposes for assessing the achievement of teacher candidates are articulated, identifying the formative and summative decisions to be made on the basis of assessment results.
- All relevant achievement targets are spelled out in standards of teacher competence to be mastered by candidates, with each standard deconstructed into its relevant scaffolding and then transformed into candidate-friendly language, coupled with samples of evidence of strong and weak work.

- All faculty members are sufficiently assessment literate to devise quality assessments of candidate achievement that produce accurate results.
- Record keeping and communication systems are in place to deliver results to intended users in a timely and understandable form.
- Teacher candidates are welcomed into the formative classroom assessment, record keeping, and communication processes during their learning.

I will analyze each of these in more detail for the teacher preparation context.

Key 1: Clear Purposes

In this context, at least four sets of decisions can be informed by assessment results, each associated with a different decision maker and being formative in nature.

Pupils need evidence about their own academic development over time in order to make decisions about their needs and to plan their use of the resources that are available to them. This is very much a formative assessment context. Pupils need to know the levels of achievement they are expected to attain, where they are now in relation to those expectations, and what it will take to close the gap.

Faculty members need access to information about their pupils' achievement in order to diagnose the instructional needs of individual pupils and groups. This is the formative part of their assessment work. This means that some assessment results may be unique to an individual pupil, while some will need to be comparable for all pupils. Faculty members need these kinds of evidence to evaluate the efficacy of the instructional interventions that they plan and implement. Only then can they make the adjustments needed to accommodate the diverse needs of their pupils.

Beyond these types of decisions, program administrators must judge the quality of their program as a whole, determining whether the teachers being graduated can put all of the pieces together in the classroom. They need a complete set of indicators of competence for each individual pupil in order to be able to compare each pupil's evidence with preestablished standards to determine if they have mastered what it takes to be a teacher.

Key 2: Clear Targets

To begin with, teacher education faculties must establish the ultimate standards to be attained by teacher candidates by the end of the program in order to assure their preparedness to teach. Then the faculty must deconstruct their standards into the appropriate scaffolding—that is, develop a teacher training curriculum that will unfold over time to bring candidates to ultimate competence. Effective assessment practices can then serve the formative purpose of helping candidates and faculty track progress toward ultimate success and the summative purpose of proving that candidates have arrived there.

The building blocks of teacher competence break down into the same categories as those of other disciplines. For example, several domains of knowledge form the foundation of the ability to teach effectively. To begin with, one must be a confident, competent master of the academic discipline(s) or content areas that he or she plans to teach. In addition, a specific knowledge of pedagogy is required, knowledge of theories of learning, child development, teaching methods, the principles of sound formative and summative assessment, and classroom management techniques, to mention just a few. In each case, there are enduring theories, generalizations or principles, and concepts that teachers need to understand. The point is that there is an important knowledge base that underpins success as a teacher, which candidates must master and faculties must assess along the way. By doing this well, faculties of education can model this key facet of sound assessment practice for their candidates.

Further, graduates must learn when and how to apply their knowledge to benefit pupil learning. For example, one must be proficient at analytical reasoning to be able to conduct task analyses of learning requirements—that is, to break down learning for pupils into manageable chunks. It is important to be able to reason comparatively, to draw inductive and deductive inferences, and to synthesize concepts and ideas in order to promote understanding. Without doubt, effective teachers are proficient critical thinkers—they can make and defend judgments through the effective application of appropriate criteria. Further, they can assemble this variety of reasoning patterns in any context and, at a moment's notice, can generate solutions to complex classroom problems.

Thus, these patterns of reasoning underpin success in teaching. Teacher preparation programs must provide opportunities for candidates to learn them. In addition, if these patterns do represent important prerequisites to effective teaching, then faculties of education must be in a position to define those learning targets clearly, blend them into instruction, and assess candidate mastery of them—both formatively and summatively. This is part of the challenge of improving assessment practice and of enhancing assessment training in teacher preparation.

Obviously, effective teachers rely on certain performance skills—that is, interactive behaviors required to help pupils learn. These are the kinds of things one can see in teaching performance if one videotapes a teacher in action. They include verbal skills, interpersonal interaction skills, and the use of various forms of media during the teaching process. If these performance skills are indeed essential for good teaching, then the faculty of education must be prepared to assess their quality and use assessment results to help candidates grow and to ensure competence. There also are teaching-related products that underpin good teaching and that must therefore meet certain standards of quality. These represent tangible products that are created by the teacher but that exist independently of that teacher and provide evidence of proficiency. In this case, it is the responsibility of the teacher education faculty to identify those key products and to be prepared to determine through rigorous assessment that their graduates are capable of creating them.

Finally, successful teachers develop certain attitudes, values, interests, preferences, and motivations—that is, dispositions that prepare them to fulfill the responsibilities of a teacher. Dispositions vary in their focus, direction, and intensity. One develops attitudes about things such as pupils, colleagues, formative assessment, or particular school subjects. One also values certain kinds of learning or certain kinds of pupil behavior. In all cases, dispositions are directed at someone or something, and are directional. We can have positive or negative attitudes along a continuum. We can have strong or weak values, interests, or preferences. Finally, dispositions can vary in their intensity from very positive to somewhat positive to somewhat negative or very negative.

Teacher education faculties need to establish the specific dispositions that they expect their graduates to develop and demonstrate in order to be confident that they are ready to teach. For instance, we want strong positive attitudes about the power of formative assessment. The systematic assessment of those dispositions would be needed to promote and verify the desired learning.

By modeling the clear specifications of appropriate achievement targets, faculties of education reveal to their pupils the benefits of carefully articulating their knowledge, reasoning, skill, product, and disposition expectations. Those benefits include increased efficiency for teacher and pupil, increased sense of efficacy for both, and, of course, the potential for the development of quality assessments that accurately reflect pupil achievement and serve their intended purposes.

Key 3: Accurate Assessments

With the above achievement standards in hand, along with scaffolding in place leading up to each standard, the foundation is set for the formative assessment of candidate progress and the summative assessment of qualifications to teach. The next challenge in assessment systems development is the transformation of those achievement expectations into the exercises and scoring schemes that will comprise the assessments of achievement. As mentioned previously, the development of accurate assessments requires:

- the careful selection of proper assessment methods to assure a match to the intended target(s);
- assembly of high-quality assessment exercises and scoring guides;
- representative sampling of the relevant domains of candidate achievement; and
- the development, administration, and interpretation of assessments in order to minimize bias.

In effect, for every course they teach, each faculty member must understand how a particular set of achievement expectations fits into the total curriculum that leads to ultimate success for teacher candidates. What specific enduring understandings, reasoning proficiencies, performance skills, product development capabilities, or dispositions do their candidates need to master? Once these questions are answered, then the instructor's responsibility is to devise an assessment plan for the course that will yield dependable information for them and their candidates on how everyone is progressing on the journey to excellence, as well as dependable evidence to tell them when they arrived.

In addition, all of this will be most easily and effectively managed by faculty members and their candidates with the application of formative assessment procedures that provide for deep pupil involvement in the assessment, record keeping, and communication processes.

If prospective teachers do not learn these lessons about standards of excellence in formative and summative assessment, then faculties of teacher education place the pupils of their graduates at a disadvantage. Those pupils and their families face the prospect of the ongoing mismeasurement of their achievement, along with all of the predictable consequences of that. On the other hand, if new teachers come into the classroom with knowledge of and proficiency in implementing pupil-involved assessment procedures, then they carry with them tools that have been proven to maximize both the confidence and achievement of their pupils. To reiterate, these can be taught and learned through modeling by teacher education faculty.

Key 4: Effective Communication

In teacher preparation programs, two interrelated assessment information management and communication systems are needed, one formative and the other summative.

The formative system facilitates communication during the learning process. Each candidate needs continuous access to dependable information on how he or she is doing in climbing the scaffolding that leads up to each relevant standard of teaching competence. This can take the form of formative or growth portfolios, one being built within each course as it is completed. Evidence accumulated from repeated self-assessments would reflect improvements in the candidate's capabilities. Each entry might be a source of formative feedback on how to do better the next time.

At the end of the course experience, the final assessment would provide compelling evidence of the mastery of the standards around which the course was built. These might be accumulated in a separate competence portfolio—a summative collection to be presented to the faculty by the candidate, providing compelling evidence of having met all of the program requirements.

Each assessment connects candidates and faculty members, but in different ways and for different purposes. Note, however, that to work most effectively in the teacher preparation context, both systems are best managed by the candidate, not the faculty. The faculty's job is to be sure that each candidate has access to dependable information about her or his mastery of important achievement targets, first for formative and then for summative purposes.

PROVIDING LEADERSHIP FOR FORMATIVE ASSESSMENT

Teachers cannot fulfill their formative assessment responsibilities without specific support from their administrators. They need two kinds of support systems. First, the school district must put certain conditions in place that support sound assessment practices. Second, in order for that work to be done, people in building and district administrative positions must bring certain assessment leadership competencies to the table.

District Conditions

In this case, we can divide the challenge into five parts (Chappuis, Stiggins, Arter, & Chappuis, 2005). Each contributes to the establishment of an organizational foundation for excellence in formative assessment.

First, the district must have its achievement expectations in order to provide clear, complete, and appropriate definitions of what is to be taught, learned, and assessed. State standards must be arrayed in a manner that maps each pupil's learning trajectory across grades over time. Then, leaders must be sure that every teacher is a competent, confident master of the achievement standards that his or her pupils are expected to master. Next, each standard must be deconstructed into the scaffolding that pupils will climb as they reach for each standard. Finally, these classroom level targets need to be transformed into pupil- and family-friendly versions to share from the beginning of the learning process.

Second, the district must coordinate its assessment systems in such a manner as to serve the information needs of decision makers at all relevant levels. That means systems must be in place to assure the proper collection, management, and delivery of information on pupil achievement that is tailored for use at policy, instructional support, and classroom levels (as described earlier).

Third, the district must take responsibility for assuring the accuracy of assessment evidence throughout the district. This requires both (1) assuring the formative assessment literacy of all instructional personnel, either by the application of proper hiring criteria, professional development, or proper ongoing modeling and supervision; and (2) the periodic evaluation of the assessments being used at each level to assure the dependability of results.

Fourth, the district must assure that effective communication systems are in place for delivering assessment results into the hands of the intended users in a timely and understandable manner. This assurance needs to apply whether communication is formative to support learning within the classroom or summative by means of test scores, report card grades, standards-based communications, portfolios, or conferences.

Finally, if policy guides practice, both district and building policy manuals and their associated regulations must be reviewed to verify that the policies found there guide sound formative assessment practices. This includes curriculum, assessment, communication, resource allocation, and personnel among other policies.

Leader Competencies

Given these responsibilities and the other challenges framed above, people in curriculum and instructional leadership positions must bring with them a clearly defined set of assessment competencies (Chappuis et al., 2005). Specifically, each leader must:

- understand the standards of accurate pupil assessment and how to meet each standard in all relevant assessment contexts;
- understand the principles of formative assessment used to support learning and how to work with staff to integrate them into instruction;
- understand the need for clear academic standards that are aligned to classroom targets and how these underpin accurate assessment;
- be able to evaluate teachers' classroom assessment competencies and to help teachers learn to assess accurately and use the results productively in formative and summative ways;
- plan, present, or secure professional development experiences that contribute to sound formative assessment practices;
- analyze pupil achievement data accurately, use the results to improve instruction, and assist teachers in doing the same;

- develop and implement sound assessment-related policies;
- create conditions necessary for the appropriate reporting and use of pupil achievement information, and communicate effectively with all members of the school community about assessment results and their implications;
- understand the attributes of sound and balanced formative and summative assessment systems; and
- understand the issues related to the unethical and inappropriate use of assessment, and protect pupils and staff from such misuses.

(p. 99)

If school leaders are to assist in conquering the formative assessment frontier, then their preservice training programs must begin to lay a foundation among these competencies, with in-service professional development following up with ongoing professional learning.

EDUCATING COMMUNITIES, SCHOOL BOARDS, AND LEGISLATORS

Policy makers have been driven by the belief that high-stakes testing is good for all pupils because such tests motivate learning. They have "raised the bar" to "world-class standards" in order to introduce "greater rigor" into the curriculum, based on the inherent belief that you get more learning by demanding it. The final challenge we face is to help policy makers understand that the development of effective schools is just not that simple.

The challenge is to help policy makers and community leaders expand the scope of their vision of excellence in formative assessment. They need to understand the concept of balanced formative and summative assessment. They must understand that, if the objective is to maximize learning, we must:

- back our high-stakes summative tests up with classroom-level formative assessment environments that help all pupils not only to believe that success is within reach but actually to succeed,
- build comprehensive assessment local systems that honor the information needs of all assessment users—formative and summative—not just the adults who make summative decisions once a year, and
- provide all educators with the opportunity to learn how to use assessment in formative ways that support—and don't just grade—pupil learning.

We know what teachers and school leaders need to know and understand to succeed in using assessment as a school improvement tool. We also know what will happen to pupil achievement if teachers do the right things by way of balanced assessment and high-quality formative assessment. We even know how to deliver relevant, helpful formative assessment tools into teachers' hands in an effective and efficient manner by means of professional learning communities. The only remaining question is whether teachers and administrators will be given the opportunity to learn to apply sound formative assessment practices. Historically, the answer to that final question has been no. That answer is no longer acceptable.

SUMMARY AND CONCLUSIONS

During this bicentennial celebration of Lewis and Clark's journey of discovery, we need leaders who, like President Thomas Jefferson, are prepared to equip pioneers with the resources they need to explore and conquer this final assessment frontier: formative applications in the classroom. In this case, the resources needed are time to learn about sound practices and work environments governed by policies and supervision that permit them to apply what they have learned. To review, the specific challenges we face are these:

1. We must build our assessment environments around the new mission of maximizing pupil achievement, not merely ranking pupils dependably by the end of high school.
2. All assessments, including those that are developed or selected and used by teachers and their pupils day-to-day in the classroom to support learning, must produce dependable results that accurately reflect pupil achievement.
3. We must use the classroom assessment process and its results to promote, not merely to monitor and grade, pupil achievement.
4. Teachers must be given the opportunity to learn about sound formative assessment practices, a facet of professional practice that has historically not been included in the preservice preparation.
5. School leaders must be given the opportunity to understand the differences between sound and unsound assessment practices—again, historically a major gap in their professional preparation.
6. Finally, if policy guides practice, then we need policies at the classroom, building, district, state, and federal levels to be developed and implemented by school and community leaders who understand the differences between sound and unsound practices and their impact on pupil learning as described above and throughout this volume.

Pioneers equipped with these resources can turn the formative assessment process, which by and large remains an unsolved mystery to most practitioners, into a powerful ally in the service of pupil success.

REFERENCES

Black, P., & Wiliam, D. (1998). Assessment and classroom learning. *Educational Assessment: Principles, Policy and Practice, 5*(1), 7–74.

Bloom, B. (1984). The search for methods of group instruction as effective as one-to-one tutoring. *Educational Leadership, 41*(8), 4–17.

Chappuis, S., Stiggins, R., Arter, J., & Chappuis, J. (2005). *Assessment FOR Learning: An Action Guide for School Leaders (*2nd Ed.). Portland, OR: Assessment Training Institute.

Meisels, S., Atkins-Burnett, S., Xue, Y., & Bickel, D. D. (2003). Creating a system of accountability: The impact of instructional assessment on elementary children's achievement scores. *Educational Policy Analysis Archives, 11*(9). Retrieved from http://epaa.asu.edu/eapp/v11n9/ February 28, 2003.

Rodriguez, M. C. (2004). The role of classroom assessment in pupil performance on TIMSS. *Applied Measurement in Education, 17*(1), 1–24.

Stiggins, R., Arter, J., Chappuis, J., & Chappuis, S. (2004). *Classroom Assessment FOR Pupil Learning: Doing It Right—Using It Well*. Portland, OR: Assessment Training Institute.

CHAPTER 3

A Theoretical Foundation for Formative Assessment

Dylan Wiliam & Siobhan Leahy

Improving pupil learning should be a priority for any society. Increasing the level of educational achievement brings benefits both to the individual, such as higher lifetime earnings, and also to society as a whole, in terms of increased economic growth and lower social costs such as health care and criminal justice costs (Hanushek, 2004). The total return on investments in education can be well over $10 for every $1 invested (Schweinhart, Montie, Xiang, Barnett, Belfield, & Nores, 2005). Even poorly focused investments in education are likely to be cost-effective to society as a whole, but given public skepticism about such investments and the reluctance of governments at local, state, and federal levels to raise taxes, there is a pressing need to find the most cost-effective ways to improve pupil achievement. We argue here that the *most* cost-effective way to improve pupil achievement is through developing teachers' ability to use assessment to adapt their instruction to meet pupil learning needs in real time—sometimes called "formative assessment" or "assessment for learning." We present a theoretical framework that identifies five key strategies. We then show how this framework can, in turn, be integrated with instructional design through a focus on the regulation of learning processes to better meet pupil needs. In this chapter, we summarize the research on the use of assessment to support learning and indicate how the key ideas of formative assessment can be integrated within the broader theoretical framework of the regulation of learning processes.

WHEN IS ASSESSMENT FORMATIVE?

Stiggins and Bridgeford (1985) found that, although many teachers created their own assessments, "in at least a third of the structured performance assessment created by these teachers, important assessment procedures appeared not to be followed" (p. 282) and "in an average of 40% of the structured performance assessments, teachers rely on mental record-keeping" (p. 283). A few years later, two substantial review articles, one by Natriello (1987) and the other by Crooks (1988), provided clear evidence that classroom evaluation practices had substantial impact on pupils and their learning, although that impact was rarely beneficial. However, the difficulty of reviewing relevant research in this area was highlighted by Black and Wiliam (1998b) in their synthesis of research published since the reviews by Natriello and Crooks. Those two sources had cited 91 and 241 references respectively, and yet only nine references were common to both papers. In their own research, Black and Wiliam (1998a) resorted to manual searches of 76 journals between 1987 and 1997 that were considered most likely to contain relevant research. Black and Wiliam's review (which cited 250 studies) found that effective use of classroom assessment yielded improvements in pupil achievement between 0.4 and 0.7 standard deviations. A more recent review focusing on studies in higher education (Nyquist, 2003) found similar results.

Over thirty years ago, Bloom (1969) suggested that "evaluation in relation to the process of learning and teaching can have strong positive effects on the actual learning of pupils as well as on their motivation for the learning and their self-concept in relation to school learning" (p. 50). It is now safe to conclude that the question has been settled: Attention to classroom assessment practices can indeed have a substantial impact on pupil achievement (see Chapter 4). What is less clear is what exactly constitutes effective classroom assessment, and how the gains in pupil achievement that the research shows are possible can be achieved at scale.

Educational assessments are conducted in a variety of ways, and their outcomes can be used for a variety of purposes. There are also differences in the purposes that assessments serve. Broadly, educational assessments serve three functions:

- to support learning (formative)
- to certify the achievements or potential of individuals (summative)
- to evaluate the quality of educational institutions, programs or curricula (evaluative)

In broad terms, moving from formative through summative to evaluative functions of assessment requires data at increasing levels of aggregation, from the individual to the institution and from specifics of particular skills and weaknesses to generalities about overall levels of performance. Of course, evaluative data may still be disaggregated in order to identify specific subgroups in the population that are not making progress, or to identify particular weaknesses in pupils' performance in specific areas, as is the case in France (Black & Wiliam, 2005.) However, it is also clear that the different functions that assessments may serve are in tension. Because of the practice of "teaching to the test," the use of data from assessments to hold schools accountable has, in many cases, rendered the data almost useless for attesting to the qualities of individual pupils (apart, of course, from those qualities that are tested) or for supporting learning.

In the United States, the term *formative assessment* is often used to describe assessments that are used to provide information on the likely performance of pupils on state-mandated tests—a usage that might better be described as "early-warning summative." In other contexts, it is used to describe any feedback given to pupils, no matter what use is made of it, such as telling pupils which items they got correct and incorrect (sometimes called "knowledge of results"). These kinds of usages suggest that the distinction between *formative* and *summative* applies to the assessments themselves, but since the same assessment can be used both formatively and summatively, these terms are more usefully applied to the use to which the information arising from assessments is put.

For the purpose of this chapter, then, the qualifier *formative* will refer not to an assessment or even to the purpose of an assessment, but rather to the function that it actually serves. An assessment is formative to the extent that information from the assessment is fed back within the system and actually used to improve the performance of the system in some way (i.e., that the assessment *forms* the direction of the improvement).

So, for example, if a pupil is told that she needs to work harder and does work harder as a result, and, consequently, does indeed make improvements in her performance, this would *not* be formative. The feedback would be *causal*, since it did trigger the improvement in performance, but not *formative*, because decisions about *how* to "work harder" were left to the pupil. Telling pupils to "give more detail" might be formative, but only if the pupils know what giving more detail means (which is unlikely, because if they knew the amount of detail required, they would probably have provided it in the first place). Similarly, a "formative assessment" that predicts which pupils are likely to fail the forthcoming state-mandated test is not formative unless the information from the test can be used to improve the quality of the learning within the system. To be formative, feedback needs to contain an implicit or explicit recipe for future action.

According to Ramaprasad (1983), a defining feature of feedback is that it has an impact on the performance of the system. Information that does not have the capability to improve the performance of the system is not feedback:

"Feedback is information about the gap between the actual level and the reference level of a system parameter which is used to alter the gap in some way" (Ramaprasad, 1983, p. 4).

In this view, formative assessments (or *feedback*, in Ramaprasad's terminology) cannot be separated from their instructional consequences, and assessments are formative only to the extent that they impact learning (for an extended discussion on consequences as the key part of the validity of formative assessments, see Wiliam and Black, 1996). The other important feature of Ramaprasad's (1983) definition is that it draws attention to three key instructional processes:

- establishing where the learners are in their learning
- establishing where they are going
- establishing what needs to be done to get them there

Traditionally, this may have been seen as the teacher's job, but it is also necessary to take account of the role that the learners themselves, and their peers, play in these processes. Crossing the three instructional processes with the different agents (teacher, peer, learner) suggests the framework shown in Figure 3.1, which indicates that formative assessment can be conceptualized as consisting of five key strategies. The "big idea" that integrates these five key strategies is that evidence about pupil learning is used to adjust instruction to better meet pupil needs—in other words, teaching is *adaptive* to the pupil's learning needs.

Details on how teachers have used these strategies to implement assessment for learning in their classrooms can be found in Leahy, Lyon, Thompson, and Wiliam (2005). In the remainder of this chapter, we discuss how formative assessment can be integrated theoretically with instructional design through the more general idea of the regulation of learning processes.

FORMATIVE ASSESSMENT AND
THE REGULATION OF LEARNING

Although the starting point for work on formative assessment was the relatively simple idea of feedback, the formulation above presents rather a complex picture of formative assessment, and the ways in which the elements within Figure 3.1 relate to each other are not straightforward. However, all the elements in Figure 3.1 can be integrated within the more general theoretical framework of the regulation of learning processes as suggested by Perrenoud (1991, 1998). The word *regulation* has an unfortunate connotation in English, stemming from the idea of "rules and regulations." In French, there are two ways to translate the word *regulation—règlement* and *régulation*.

Figure 3.1. Five Key Strategies in Formative Assessment

	Where the Learner Is Going	Where the Learner Is Right Now	How to Get There
Teacher	**1** Clarifying learning intentions and criteria for success	**2** Engineering effective classroom discussions and tasks that elicit evidence of learning	**3** Providing feedback that moves learners forward
Peer	Understanding learning intentions and criteria for success	**4** Activating students as instructional resources for one another	
Learner	Understanding learning intentions and criteria for success	**5** Activating students as the owners of their learning	

The former has the connotation of rules and regulations, while the latter connotes adjustment—for example, in the way that a thermostat regulates the temperature of a room. It is the latter sense in which the word is used in the idea of the regulation of learning, and although the term *regulation* is not ideal for describing this meaning in English, in this chapter, we will continue to use it, mainly because there is no suitable alternative.

Within such a framework, the actions of the teacher, the learners, and the context of the classroom are all evaluated with respect to the extent to which they contribute to guiding the learning toward the intended goal. In this context, it is important to note that teachers do not create learning; only learners can create learning. In the past, this fact has resulted in calls for a shift in the role of the teacher from the "sage on the stage" to the "guide on the side." The danger with such a characterization is that it is often interpreted as relieving the teacher of responsibility for ensuring that learning takes place. What we propose here is that the teacher be regarded as responsible for "engineering" a learning environment, both in its design and its operation.

Pupil Engagement

The key features of an effective learning environment are that it creates pupil engagement and that it is well regulated. A growing body of research on cognitive development shows that the level of engagement in cognitively challenging environments influences not only achievement, but also IQ (Dickens and Flynn, 2001). As well as creating engagement, however, effective learning environments need to be designed so that, as far as possible, they afford, or scaffold, the learning that is intended (*proactive* regulation). The learning environment should also ensure that if the intended learning is not occurring, then this becomes apparent, so appropriate adjustments may be made (*interactive* regulation).

The first thing to say here is that it is important to distinguish between the regulation of the activity in which the pupil engages and the regulation of the learning that results. Most teachers appear to be quite skilled at the former but have only a hazy idea of the learning that results. For example, when asked, "What are your learning intentions for this lesson?" many teachers reply by saying something like, "I'm going to have them describe a friend," which conflates the learning intention with the activity (Clarke, 2003). In a way, this is understandable, since only the activities can be manipulated directly. Nevertheless, it is clear that in teachers who have developed their formative assessment practices, there is a strong shift in emphasis away from regulating the activities in which pupils engage and toward the learning that results (Black, Harrison, Lee, Marshall, & Wiliam, 2003).

Proactive Regulation

Proactive regulation is achieved proactively (i.e., before the lesson begins), through the setting up of "didactical situations" (Brousseau, 1984). The regulation can be unmediated within such didactical situations, when, for example, a teacher "does not intervene in person, but puts in place a 'metacognitive culture', mutual forms of teaching and the organisation of regulation of learning processes run by technologies or incorporated into classroom organisation and management" (Perrenoud, 1998, p. 100). For example, a teacher's decision to use realistic contexts in the mathematics classroom can provide a source of regulation, because pupils can then determine the reasonableness of their answers. If pupils calculate, for example, that the average cost of a slice of pizza is $200, if they are genuinely engaged in the activity, they will know that this solution is unreasonable. Therefore, the use of realistic settings provides a "self-checking" mechanism. Similarly, if a teacher spends time creating a culture in the classroom in which pupils are used to consulting and supporting each other in productive ways, then this contributes to keeping the learning "on track."

Proactive Planning

On the other hand, the didactical situation may be set up so that the regulation is achieved through the mediation of the teacher—*interactive* regulation —when the teacher, in planning the lesson, creates questions, prompts, or activities that evoke responses from the pupils that the teacher can use to determine the progress of the learning, and if necessary, to make adjustments. Examples of such questions include: "Is calculus exact or approximate?", "What is the pH of 10 molar NaOH?", and "Would your mass be the same on the moon?" (It is worth noting that each of these questions is "closed"— there is only one correct response. Their value is that although they are closed, each question focuses on a specific misconception.)

Proactive planning creates, interactively, the possibility that the learning activities may change course in the light of the pupils' responses. These "moments of contingency"—points in the instructional sequence when the instruction can proceed in different directions according to the way pupils respond—are at the heart of the regulation of learning.

These moments arise continuously in whole-class teaching, where teachers must constantly make sense of pupils' responses, interpreting them in terms of learning needs and making appropriate responses. They also arise when the teacher circulates around the classroom, looking at individual pupils' work and observing the extent to which the pupils are "on track." In most teaching of mathematics and science, the regulation of learning will be relatively tight. The teacher will attempt to "bring into line" all learners who are not heading toward the particular goal sought by the teacher—in these subjects, the *telos* of learning is generally both highly specific and common to all the pupils in a class. In contrast, in the teaching of language arts and social studies, the regulation will be much looser. Rather than a single goal, there is likely to be a broad *horizon* of appropriate goals, all of which are acceptable, and the teacher will intervene to bring the learners "into line" only when the trajectory of the learner is radically different from that intended by the teacher. Having said this, where a class is considering the ethical impact of scientific discoveries or pursuing a mathematical investigation, the regulation is likely to be more like that in the typical language arts classroom. Conversely, where the teacher is teaching the conventions of grammar, the regulation is likely to be much tighter, since the goal is to teach all pupils to use the same conventions.

Formative Lessons

One of the features that makes a lesson "formative," then, is that the lesson can change course in the light of evidence about the progress of learning. This is in stark contrast to the "traditional" pattern of classroom interaction, where little is contingent on the responses of the pupils, except how long it takes to get to the next part of the teacher's "script," so there is little scope for *interactive* regulation. The teacher treats all incorrect responses as equivalent in terms of information content; all the teacher learns is that the pupils didn't "get" it. This is typical in situations where the questions that the teacher uses in whole-class interaction have not been prepared in advance (in other words, when there is little or no *proactive* regulation).

Similar considerations apply when the teacher collects in the pupils' notebooks and attempts to give helpful feedback in the form of comments on how to improve, rather than grades or percentage scores. If sufficient attention has not been given proactively to the design of the tasks the pupils are asked to do, then the teacher may find that he or she has nothing useful to say to the pupils. Ideally, from examining the pupils' responses to the task, the teacher would be able to judge (a) how to help the learners learn better, and (b) what he or she might do to improve the teaching of the topic to a future class, thus providing a third form of regulation—*retroactive* regulation. In this way, the assessment could be formative for the pupils, through the feedback the teacher provides, and formative for the teacher in that appropriate analysis of the pupils' responses might suggest how the lesson could be improved for other pupils.

Assessments can also be formative at the level of the school, district, and state, provided that the assessments help to regulate learning. Frequent assessment can identify those pupils who are not making as much progress as expected (whether this expectation is based on some notion of "ability," prior achievement, or external demands made by the state). But frequent summative testing—we might call this "microsummative"—is not formative unless the information that the tests yield is used in some way to modify instruction.

FEEDBACK LOOPS

A key issue in the design of assessment systems, if they are to function formatively as well as summatively, is the extent to which the system can respond in a timely manner to the information made available. In designing feedback loops, it is necessary to take into account the responsiveness of the system to the actions that can be used to improve its performance. The less responsive the system, the longer the feedback loops need to be for the system to be able to react appropriately.

For example, analysis of the patterns of pupil responses on a trial run of a state-mandated test in a given school district might indicate that the responses made by seventh-grade pupils on items involving probability were lower than would be expected given the pupils' scores on the other items, and lower than the scores of comparable pupils in other districts. One response to this might be a program of professional development on teaching probability for the seventh-grade mathematics teachers in the district. Since this would take weeks to arrange—and even longer to have an effect—the trial run would need to be held some months before the state-mandated test in order to provide time for the system to interpret the data in terms of the system's needs. The trial run would be formative for the district if, and only if, the information generated were used to improve the performance of the system—and if the data from the assessment actually helped to direct the action taken.

For an individual teacher, feedback loops can be considerably shorter. A teacher might look through the same pupils' responses to a trial run of a state test and replan the topics that she is going to teach in the time remaining before the test. Such a trial run would be useful as little as a week or two before the state-mandated test, as long as there is time to use the information to redirect the teaching. Again, this assessment would be formative as long as the information from the test was actually used to adapt the teaching, telling the teacher which topics need to be retaught and suggesting what kinds of reteaching might produce better results.

The building-in of time for responses is a central feature of much elementary and middle school teaching in Japan. For example, in middle-school science, a teaching unit is typically allocated 14 lessons, but the content usually occupies only 10 or 11 of the lessons, allowing time for a short test to be given in the 12th lesson, and for the teacher to reteach aspects of the unit that were not well understood in lessons 13 and 14.

Another example, on an even shorter time scale, is the use of "exit passes" from a lesson. The idea here is that before leaving a classroom, each pupil must compose an answer to a key question given by the teacher at the end of the lesson. For a lesson on probability, for example, such a question might be, "Why can't a probability be greater than one?" Once the pupils have left, the teacher can look at their responses and make appropriate adjustments in planning the next period of instruction.

The shortest feedback loops are those involved in the day-to-day classroom practices of teachers, where teachers adjust their teaching in light of pupils' responses to questions or other prompts in "real time." The key point is that the length of the feedback loop should be tailored according to the ability of the system to react to the feedback.

However, this does not mean that the responsiveness of the system cannot be changed. Through appropriate proactive regulation, responsiveness can be enhanced considerably. Where teachers have collaborated to anticipate the responses that pupils might make to a question and what misconceptions would lead to particular incorrect responses—for example, through the process of Lesson Study practiced in Japan (Lewis, 2002)—the teachers would be able to adapt their instruction much more quickly. They might even have alternative instructional episodes ready. In this way, feedback to the teacher that, in the normal course of things, might need at least a day to be used to modify instruction, could affect instruction immediately.

In the same way, a school district or state that has thought about how it might use information about pupil performance before the pupils' results are available (for example, by preparing particular kinds of diagnostic reports; see Wiliam, 1999) is likely to reduce considerably the time needed to use the information to improve instruction. As in other examples, attention to *proactive* regulation pays dividends *interactively*.

All this suggests that the conflicting uses of the term *formative assessment* can be reconciled by recognizing that all assessments can be formative, as long as they are used to make instructional adjustments, but that a crucial difference between assessments is the length of the adjustment cycle. A terminology for the different lengths of cycles is given in Table 3.1.

Although this theoretical perspective allows us to regard assessments using a range of different cycle lengths, all of which are considered potentially formative, the research evidence available to date suggests that not all cycle lengths are equally powerful. The longer the cycle, the more remote the action to adjust instruction will be from the situation in which the original evidence was elicited. Long cycle assessments can be used to align curriculum or to improve instruction for subsequent pupils, but they generally have only limited impact on pupil achievement. The empirical evidence assembled in the reviews of the literature cited above suggest that short cycle formative assessment has the greatest impact on pupil achievement.

PUTTING RESEARCH INTO PRACTICE

No matter how elegantly we formulate our ideas about formative assessment, they will be moot unless we can find ways to support teachers in incorporating more attention to assessment into their own practice. If educational research is to have any lasting impact on practice, it must be taken up and used by practitioners. Traditionally, researchers have engaged in a process of disseminating their work to teachers, or engaging in knowledge transfer. Both of these processes have some utility, but they suggest that all researchers need to do is to "share the results" (English, Jones, Lesh, Tirosh, & Bussi, 2002, p. 805) of their research with practitioners and the findings will somehow be used.

However, the emerging research shows that the process of knowledge transfer cannot be one of providing instructions to novices in the hope that

Table 3.1. Types of Formative Assessment

Type	Focus	Length
Long-cycle	Between instructional units	Four weeks to one year
Medium-cycle	Between lessons	One day to two weeks
Short-cycle	Within a single lesson	Five seconds to one hour

they will get better (see Wiliam, 2003), because, put simply, all research findings are generalizations and as such are either too general to be useful or too specific to be universally applicable. For example, the research on feedback suggests that feedback ought to be task-involving rather than ego-involving (Kluger & DeNisi, 1996) but what the teacher needs to know is, "Can I say, 'Well done' to this pupil now?" Put crudely, such generalizations underdetermine action.

At the other extreme, experts can often see that a particular recipe is inappropriate in some circumstances, but because their reaction is intuitive, they may not be able to discern the reason why. The message received by the practitioner in such cases is that the findings of educational research are not a valid guide to action.

The difficulty of putting research into practice is the fault of neither the teacher nor the researcher. Because our understanding of the theoretical principles underlying successful classroom action is weak, research cannot tell teachers what to do. Indeed, given the complexity of classrooms, it seems likely that the positivist dream of an effective theory of teacher action—which would spell out the "best" course of action given certain conditions—is not just difficult and a long way off, but impossible in principle (Wiliam, 2003).

What is needed instead is an acknowledgment that what teachers do in "taking on" research is not a more or less passive adoption of some good ideas from someone else but an active process of knowledge *creation*:

> Teachers will not take up attractive sounding ideas, albeit based on extensive research, if these are presented as general principles which leave entirely to them the task of translating them into everyday practice—their classroom lives are too busy and too fragile for this to be possible for all but an outstanding few. What they need is a variety of living examples of implementation, by teachers with whom they can identify and from whom they can both derive conviction and confidence that they can do better, and see concrete examples of what doing better means in practice. (Black and Wiliam, 1998b, p. 15)

CONCLUSIONS

In this paper, we have argued that the terms *formative* and *summative* apply not to assessments themselves, but to the functions they serve. As a result, the same assessment can be both formative and summative. Assessment is formative when the information arising from the assessment is fed back within the system and is actually used to improve the performance of the system. Assessment is formative:

- for individuals when they can use the feedback from the assessment to improve their learning;

- for teachers when the outcomes from the assessment, appropriately interpreted, help them improve their teaching, either on specific topics, or generally; and
- for schools and districts if the information generated can be interpreted in such a way as to improve the quality of learning within the schools and districts.

The view of assessment presented here involves a shift from quality *control* to quality *assurance* in learning. Rather than teaching pupils and then, at the end of the teaching, finding out what has been learned, it seems obvious that what we should do is assess the progress of learning while it is happening, so that we can adjust the teaching if things are not working. In order to achieve this, designing the length of the cycle from evidence to action must take into account the responsiveness of the system. Some feedback loops, such as those in the classroom, will be only seconds long, while others, such as those involving districts or state systems, will last months or even years.

More generally, we have suggested that formative assessment be considered a key component of well-regulated learning environments. From this perspective, the task of the teacher is not necessarily to teach, but rather to engineer situations in which pupils can learn effectively. One way to do this is to design the environment so that the regulation is embedded within features of the environment. Alternatively, when the regulation is undertaken through the teacher's mediation, it is necessary to build opportunities for such mediation into the instructional sequence by designing episodes that will elicit pupils' thinking (proactive regulation) and to use the evidence from these probes to modify the instruction (interactive regulation).

REFERENCES

Black, P., Harrison, C., Lee, C., Marshall, B., & Wiliam, D. (2003*). Assessment for learning: Putting it into practice*. Buckingham, UK: Open University Press.

Black, P. J., & Wiliam, D. (1998a). Assessment and classroom learning. *Assessment in Education: Principles Policy and Practice*, 5(1), 7–73.

Black, P. J., & Wiliam, D. (1998b). *Inside the black box: Raising standards through classroom assessment*. London, UK: King's College London School of Education.

Black, P., & Wiliam, D. (2005). Lessons from around the world: How policies, politics and cultures constrain and afford assessment practices. *Curriculum Journal*, 16(2), 249–261.

Bloom, B. S. (1969). Some theoretical issues relating to educational evaluation. In R. W. Tyler (Ed.), *Educational evaluation: New roles, new means: The 63rd yearbook of the National Society for the Study of Education* (Part II) Vol. 69(2), (pp. 26–50). Chicago: University of Chicago Press.

Brousseau, G. (1984). The crucial role of the didactical contract in the analysis and construction of situations in teaching and learning mathematics. In H.-G. Steiner (Ed.), *Theory of mathematics education: ICME 5 topic area and miniconference* (pp. 110–119). Bielefeld, Germany: Institut für Didaktik der Mathematik der Universität Bielefeld.

Clarke, S. (2003). *Enriching feedback in the primary classroom.* London, UK: Hodder & Stoughton.

Crooks, T. J. (1988). The impact of classroom evaluation practices on pupils. *Review of Educational Research, 58*(4), 438–481.

Dickens, W. T., & Flynn, J. R. (2001). Heritability estimates versus large environmental effects: The IQ paradox resolved. *Psychological Review, 108*, 346–369.

English, L. D., Jones, G., Lesh, R., Tirosh, D., & Bussi, M. B. (2002). Future issues and directions in international mathematics education research. In L. D. English (Ed.), *Handbook of international research in mathematics education* (pp. 787–812). Mahwah, NJ: Lawrence Erlbaum Associates.

Hanushek, E. A. (2004). *Some simple analytics of school quality* (NBER working paper W10229). Washington, DC: National Bureau of Economic Research.

Kluger, A. N., & DeNisi, A. (1996). The effects of feedback interventions on performance: A historical review, a meta-analysis, and a preliminary feedback intervention theory. *Psychological Bulletin, 119*(2), 254–284.

Leahy, S., Lyon, C., Thompson, M., & Wiliam, D. (2005). Classroom assessment: Minute-by-minute and day-by-day. *Educational Leadership, 63*(3), 19–24.

Lewis, C. C. (2002). *Lesson study: A handbook of teacher-led instructional change.* Philadelphia: Research for Better Schools.

Natriello, G. (1987). The impact of evaluation processes on pupils. *Educational Psychologist, 22*(2), 155–175.

Nyquist, J. B. (2003). *The benefits of reconstructing feedback as a larger system of formative assessment: A meta-analysis.* Unpublished master's thesis, Vanderbilt University.

Perrenoud, P. (1991). Towards a pragmatic approach to formative evaluation. In P. Weston (Ed.), *Assessment of pupil achievement* (pp. 79–101). Amsterdam, Netherlands: Swets & Zeitlinger.

Perrenoud, P. (1998). From formative evaluation to a controlled regulation of learning. Towards a wider conceptual field. *Assessment in Education: Principles Policy and Practice, 5*(1), 85–102.

Ramaprasad, A. (1983). On the definition of feedback. *Behavioral Science, 28*(1), 4–13.

Schweinhart, L. J., Montie, J., Xiang, Z., Barnett, W. S., Belfield, C. R., & Nores, M. (2005). *Lifetime effects: The High/Scope Perry Preschool Study through age 40.* Ypsilanti, MI: High/Scope Educational Research Foundation.

Stiggins, R. J., & Bridgeford, N. J. (1985). The ecology of classroom assessment. *Journal of Educational Measurement, 22*(4), 271–286.

Wiliam, D. (1999, May). *A template for computer-aided diagnostic analyses of test outcome data.* Paper presented at 25th annual conference of the International Association for Educational Assessment held at Bled, Slovenia. London, UK: King's College London School of Education.

Wiliam, D. (2003). The impact of educational research on mathematics education. In A. Bishop, M. A. Clements, C. Keitel, J. Kilpatrick, & F.K.S. Leung (Eds.), *Second International Handbook of Mathematics Education* (pp. 469–488). Dordrecht, Netherlands: Kluwer Academic Publishers.

Wiliam, D., & Black, P. J. (1996). Meanings and consequences: a basis for distinguishing formative and summative functions of assessment? *British Educational Research Journal*, 22(5), 537–548.

CHAPTER 4

Expanding Views About Formative Classroom Assessment: A Review of the Literature

Susan M. Brookhart

WHAT IS FORMATIVE ASSESSMENT?

Formative classroom assessment gives teachers information for instructional decisions and gives pupils information for improvement. Currently, the field is focusing on *pupil* use of information, sometimes called "assessment *for* learning" (Black, Harrison, Lee, Marshall, & Wiliam, 2004; Stiggins, 2005); however, formative assessment information is also useful to teachers (Bloom, Hastings, & Madaus, 1971; Stiggins, 2005).

Several definitions of formative assessment have been proposed. Taken together and seen over time, they show that the definition of formative assessment itself has been evolving. The visual organizer in Figure 4.1 oversimplifies in order to illustrate this development.

Scriven (1967) coined the terms *formative* and *summative* to refer to evaluation functions (pp. 40–43). Using evaluation in the development or improvement of an educational process is "formative." Using evaluation in decision making about the outcome of an educational process is "summative." These terms originally referred to types of evaluation, not types of assessment.

Bloom, Hastings, and Madaus (1971, p. 54) "borrowed the term 'formative evaluation' from Scriven (1967)" to refer to the brief diagnostic progress tests they used for mastery learning. In the context of mastery learning, formative evaluation gives information about pupils' progress on components of learning units or tasks. They charted a model of evaluation that began with diagnosis of relevant characteristics of the learner (including readiness, prior

Figure 4.1. Expanding Concepts in the Definition of Formative Assessment

Information About the Learning Process (Scriven, 1967)			
Information About the Learning Process (Bloom et al., 1971)	That Teachers Can Use for Instructional Decisions		
Information About the Learning Process (Sadler, 1983, 1989)	That Teachers Can Use for Instructional Decisions	And Students Can Use for Improving Their Own Performance	
Information About the Learning Process (Black & Wiliam, 1998a, 1998b; Brookhart, 1997a, 1997b; Crooks, 1988; Natriello, 1987)	That Teachers Can Use for Instructional Decisions	And Students Can Use for Improving Their Performance	Which Motivates Students

knowledge, and previous achievement). Then they proceeded to formative evaluation of components of the learning task, leading to prescriptions about what still must be learned ("feedback and corrections"; see Guskey, Chapter 5). Finally, they proceeded to summative evaluation of the extent of attainment of learning outcomes. Most of their discussion centered on the role of assessment in providing the teacher with information for instructional decisions. However, they did acknowledge the motivational value for pupils of having information along the way in the learning process.

More recently, there has been a shift to see the role of pupil more actively as the subject as well as the object of formative assessment. The term usually used now is *formative assessment*, not *formative evaluation* as per Bloom and his colleagues (1971). Black and Wiliam (1998a, 1998b) defined the core of formative assessment as two actions:

- The pupil must recognize that there is a gap between current and desired performance.
- The pupil must take effective action to close the gap.

A review of the reference sections of articles that focus on the pupil's role in formative assessment reveals that almost all of them cite Sadler (1983, 1989). Sadler (1983, p. 63) saw three steps in the formative feedback loop:

- attending to goals
- devising strategies to reach the goals
- monitoring the discrepancy between actual and desired performance

Black and Wiliam (1998b) began with pupils' recognizing a gap between actual and desired performance, and Sadler (1983) ended there. Formative assessment is truly a loop, and it is not truly "formative assessment" (that is, nothing is "formed" with it) if the feedback is not used to further pupils' learning.

THE RELATIONSHIP BETWEEN FORMATIVE AND SUMMATIVE ASSESSMENT

Crooks (1988) asked whether feedback and summative evaluation are compatible, using the term *feedback* to mean "formative assessment" (p. 457). He argued for separating the functions, reasoning that if evaluation results counted in pupil grades, for example, pupils would pay less attention to the feedback and learn less from it than if the feedback was purely for learning purposes. This is certainly the experience of many classroom teachers who find pupils centered on grades, especially as they get older (Ross, Rolheiser, & Hogaboam-Gray, 2002; Thomas & Oldfather, 1997).

Other authors point out that there need not be such a strong distinction. Formative and summative assessment can be seen as parts of the same whole (the whole being pupil learning). Whether assessment information is viewed as formative or summative depends in part on the audience and the time. From a teacher's point of view, the results of a summative end-of-unit test may be part of pupils' grades, but they also may help identify pupils who are weak in prerequisite knowledge for future learning. From a pupil's point of view, successful pupils engage in self-assessment as a regular, ongoing process and consider how summative (grade) information may inform their future careers as pupils (Brookhart, 2001).

Biggs (1998) argued that "sensible educational models make effective use of both FA [formative assessment] and SA [summative assessment]" (p. 105). Formative and summative assessment need not be mutually exclusive. The two types of assessment relate best to each other when they are "deeply criterion-referenced," that is, focused on the attributes of quality work.

I am persuaded by both logic and research that this more inclusive view is a good description of the way assessment works for learning. This literature review, as the title implies, will concentrate on literature that supports the gradually expanding view of formative assessment. However, any review of literature involves some choices about which literature to review. My inclusive view of assessment for learning allowed me to cast a broad net in the classroom assessment literature to find information that would inform an understanding of formative classroom assessment.

PREVIOUS REVIEWS OF LITERATURE

Previous reviews of literature have highlighted different aspects of classroom assessment and their effects on pupils (Bangert-Drowns, Kulik, C., & Kulik, J., 1991; Bangert-Drowns, Kulik, C., Kulik, J., & Morgan, 1991; Black & Wiliam, 1998a,b; Bloom, 1984; Blumenfeld, 1992; Brookhart, 1997a, 2004; Cicmanec & Viechnicki, 1994; Crooks, 1988; Kluger & DeNisi, 1996; Natriello, 1987; Niemi, 1997; Sadler, 1989; Shepard, 2001; Stiggins, 1999; Tittle, 1994; Traub, 1990; Wiliam & Black, 1996; Wolf, 1993).

Bloom (1984) described instruction in terms of differences in formative assessments. He described the search for methods of group instruction that are as effective as one-to-one tutoring as the "2 sigma problem" because tutoring produced an effect size of about 2 standard deviations. The fact that tutoring works, he reasoned, indicated that most pupils *can* learn regular school material, and he reviewed work by his own graduate pupils who were trying combinations of methods to see how close they could get to an effect size of 2.0. The closest study used a combination of mastery learning (Guskey, Chapter 5) and enhanced cues participation (where the teacher attended more equally to pupils), which reached an effect size of 1.7.

Natriello (1987) studied the impact of features of the evaluation processes on pupils' motivation and achievement. He concluded that these characteristics are important in classrooms: focus on tasks (not comparisons of pupils), clear criteria, high but attainable standards, cooperative reward structures, sound (from the perspective of pupils) appraisals of work, and differentiated feedback. He found that the research in many cases failed to take into account the complexity of actual classroom evaluation, where multiple purposes are often served at once and where one teacher often assesses multiple pupils as a group.

Crooks (1988) also studied the impact of classroom evaluation practices on pupils. Like Natriello, he was interested in the effects of evaluation on learning strategies, motivation, and achievement. Crooks (1988) grouped the ways in which evaluations affect pupils into short-, medium-, and long-term effects. Most relevant for formative classroom assessment is the list of short-term effects. Formative assessment (Crooks, 1988, p. 443):

- reactivates or consolidates prerequisite skills or knowledge prior to introducing new material,
- focuses attention on important aspects of the subject,
- encourages active learning strategies,

- gives pupils opportunities to practice skills and consolidate learning,
- provides knowledge of results and corrective feedback,
- helps pupils monitor their own progress and develop skills of self-evaluation,
- guides the choice of further instructional or learning activities to increase mastery, and
- helps pupils feel a sense of accomplishment.

Like Crooks, Black and Wiliam (1998a) spread a wide net, checking journals in several disciplines. They demonstrated that "formative assessment" is not a monolithic good; its use requires attention to the details of classroom and instructional context. The kind and quality of formative feedback make a difference. Nevertheless, they were able to support some general conclusions. They highlighted the importance of setting clear learning goals, choosing and articulating appropriate learning tasks, using sound pedagogy that includes feedback, and interpreting and using the feedback to guide pupil learning. Their review showed both learning and motivational benefits of pupil self-assessment and peer assessment. Black and Wiliam (1998b) also made a statement about the importance of practice by presenting a summary of their results in *Phi Delta Kappan*, under the much-quoted title "Inside the Black Box," to make their conclusions accessible to practitioners.

Shepard (2001) noted that educational tests have historically been seen as something for statisticians, and not for teachers or content specialists; conversely, conceptualizations of teaching have left out assessment. Gathering and using assessment information must become part of ongoing teaching and learning. Classroom assessment practice occurs at the intersection of three teaching functions: instruction, classroom management, and assessment (Brookhart, 2004).

The bibliography for the following review of literature includes more than 70 empirical studies and 20 reviews, plus some additional sources. Study participants included preservice teachers, in-service teachers, and/or pupils from 11 different countries. Because of the blurring of the formative and summative functions in classroom assessment, studies of general classroom assessment practices were also included. One thing that cannot be said—as some in the past were able to claim—is that there is a paucity of research in the field.

WHAT THE LITERATURE SAYS ABOUT FORMATIVE ASSESSMENT

Conventional Assessment Practices

Most classroom assessment is somewhat criterion-referenced, although the criteria are not always clear (Mavrommatis, 1997). For many teachers, grades are an important reason for assessment (Barnes, 1985; Kusch, 1999; Wilson, 1990) and limit the kind of assessment teachers do (Schmidt & Brosnan, 1996). This can actually work against formative functions: Reports "typically reaffirm judgments about achievement rather than develop them, with the result that very little alteration of instruction is made as a result of the evaluation activity" (Wilson, 1990, p. 4).

Many conventional assessment practices are logically associated with the age of pupils or the subject matter taught. Elementary school teachers use more varied assessment methods than secondary school teachers do (Gullickson, 1985; Wilson, 1990), including a large range of methods and "academic enablers" such as effort and improvement (Cizek, Fitzgerald, & Rachor, 1995; McMillan, Myran, & Workman, 2002). Primary level teachers use observation extensively (Adams & Hsu, 1998; Gipps, McCallum, & Hargreaves, 2000; Nicholson & Anderson, 1993).

Secondary teachers use fewer commercially prepared tests and more teacher-made tests, often more objective tests (Gullickson, 1985; Stiggins & Bridgeford, 1985; Stiggins & Conklin, 1992; Wilson, 1990; Zhang & Burry-Stock, 2003). They consider "academic enablers" like effort and improvement to be achievement-related constructs; this varies with the ability level of the class (Cizek, Fitzgerald, & Rachor, 1995; McMillan, 2001). Secondary social studies teachers use constructed response items more than other teachers (McMillan, 2001). Although recall questions are dominant whether teachers write their own tests (Stiggins, Griswold, & Wikelund, 1989) or whether the tests come from textbooks (Frisbie, Miranda, & Baker, 1993), teachers do sometimes use questions that tap higher-order thinking (Gullickson, 1985; Kahn, 2000; Stiggins, Griswold, & Wikelund, 1989).

Teacher Beliefs

Teacher beliefs about assessment affect assessment practices (Frary, Cross, & Weber, 1993; Mavrommatis, 1997; McMillan, 2003; Raveaud, 2004; Schmidt & Brosnan, 1996). Teacher assessment beliefs can be altered with study (Goldberg & Roswell, 1999–2000; Johnson, Wallace, & Thompson, 1999; Torrance & Pryor, 2001). Teachers do not always use available assessment information in their instructional decisions (Thomas & Oldfather, 1997). Teacher beliefs about some aspects of assessment are negative (Barnes, 1985; Brown, 2004; Frary, Cross, & Weber, 1993; Pryor & Akwesi, 1998).

For example, the 10th-grade English teachers in Kahn's (2000) case study believed it wasn't fair to use novel passages in assessments to determine achievement of general goals (e.g., pupils will be able to evaluate what they read). They were concerned about including specific literary works that had been "covered in class." Teachers believed that this traditional approach to testing was more likely to encourage pupil attention and cooperation in class.

Teachers not only felt that including new works on an assessment wasn't fair, but they also feared pupils would not pay attention in class if the specific literature was not going to be on the test. Tests therefore often simplified the understanding of subjects such as theme or symbolism and reduced them to recall items.

Classroom Assessment Environment

A classroom assessment environment exists (Raveaud, 2004; Stiggins & Conklin, 1992), and it affects pupil perceptions, performance, and behavior. Stiggins and his colleagues (Stiggins & Bridgeford, 1985; Stiggins & Conklin, 1992) described the classroom assessment environment in terms of teacher practices: assessment purposes, methods, criteria, and quality; feedback; the teacher's background in assessment and perception of pupils; and the assessment policy environment. These teacher characteristics, which define what Stiggins and Conklin (1992) termed the *classroom assessment environment*, are similar to what sociologists have termed aspects of *classroom structure* (Rosenholtz & Rosenholtz, 1981; Simpson, 1981): the level of classroom task differentiation, the amount of pupil autonomy, grouping practices, and grading practices.

These instructional and assessment choices lead to different classroom environments in which pupils "construct identities" (Rosenholtz & Rosenholtz, 1981). More unidimensional classroom structures (whole-group instruction, little pupil choice, frequent summative grading) are associated with a more normal distribution of ability perceptions and more consensus about individuals' ability levels than more multidimensional classrooms (individualized instruction, pupil choice, less frequent grading; Rosenholtz & Rosenholtz, 1981; Simpson, 1981). Natriello (1996) studied high school pupils and concluded that incompatibilities in evaluation and authority systems were strongly related to pupil disengagement from high school. Thus, the evaluation system (or assessment environment) can have negative effects on pupil behavior and performance.

Motivation and learning theories have been linked with the idea of a classroom assessment environment to frame studies of the role of classroom assessment in pupil motivation and learning (Brookhart, 1997a, 1997b, 2003; Brookhart & DeVoge, 1999; Brookhart & Durkin, 2003; Church, Elliot, & Gable, 2001). The assessment environment has an indirect effect on graded performance, mediated by pupils' achievement goals (Church, Elliot, & Gable, 2001).

Effective Formative Assessment and Feedback

Effective formative assessment blends assessment and instructional functions. Clear criteria and high-quality feedback are crucial to the process. Effective feedback compares pupil performance with known criteria in relatively frequent, manageable increments (such that the pupil improvement required is understandable and doable).

Gipps and her colleagues (Gipps, McCallum, & Hargreaves, 2000; Tunstall & Gipps, 1996) interviewed teachers of young children (years 1 and 2) and their pupils in the United Kingdom and produced a typology of the kinds of feedback that teachers give. There were two main types of feedback: for socialization and for assessment. Although the typology was developed for teachers of young children, it has more general applicability (Shepard, 2001).

Descriptive, as opposed to evaluative, feedback is more useful for the improvement of work. The nature of the description is more important than whether the feedback is positive or negative. Criticism can be useful feedback to "construct the way forward" (Tunstall & Gipps, 1996, p. 394). Formative assessment works to assist future learning by (Rea-Dickens, 2001, p. 454): 1) reducing the size of the task for the child, 2) keeping the child "in the field" and motivated, 3) marking critical or relevant features, 4) modeling an idealized version of the task, and 5) encouraging the learner to think evaluatively.

Several classroom experiments with feedback have highlighted its importance. Elawar and Corno (1985) conducted a factorial experiment on teachers' written feedback on pupil homework. Constructive criticism on errors and how to improve, coupled with at least one positive remark on what was done well, improved both pupil performance and attitude. Furthermore, teachers believed that it had this effect. Butler (1987; Butler & Nisan, 1986) also did classroom experiments with feedback with fifth and sixth graders in Israel, with similar results.

Kluger and DeNisi (1996) examined studies of the effects of feedback interventions on performance more broadly. Their theoretical argument shared Elawar and Corno's (1985) focus on attention and Sadler's (1989) focus on comparing performance to an ideal. Kluger and DeNisi (1996, p. 259) postulated that behavior is regulated by comparisons of feedback to goals or standards, which are organized hierarchically. Attention is limited, and only feedback-standard gaps that receive attention actively help regulate behavior. Attention is normally directed to a moderate level of the hierarchy (goals that are neither too broad nor too specific). Feedback interventions direct attention and therefore affect behavior.

Bangert-Drowns and his colleagues published two meta-analyses using the same set of 40 studies from basic and higher education. Bangert-Drowns, Kulik, Kulik, and Morgan (1991) analyzed the instructional effect of feedback in test-like events, theorizing that the main function of feedback was to correct errors. They found that feedback was most effective under conditions that encouraged learners' mindful reception of the content. Bangert-

Drowns, Kulik, and Kulik (1991) analyzed the effects of frequent classroom testing. They found that testing frequency in control conditions was the most important predictor of effect size between control (no feedback) and experimental conditions, suggesting that knowledge of incremental results functioned as a kind of feedback itself. Attitudes were more positive with more frequent testing. The effects of frequency of testing showed diminishing returns on achievement.

Negative Effects of Poor Classroom Assessment

Studies of teachers learning to give good feedback indicate that it is difficult to do well, and that it can have negative effects if done poorly (Bachor & Baer, 2001; Isaacson, 1999; Rea-Dickens, 2001; Torrance & Pryor, 1998). Kusch (1999) found that pupil teachers experienced cooperating teachers' pressure to maintain established classroom order. Cooperating teachers expected pupil teachers to produce grades, sanction pupil thinking, and police pupil behavior. Assessment did not really tell pupil teachers how to adjust lessons.

Similarly, when they studied New Zealand primary teachers who were teaching about technology (computers), Moreland and Jones (2000) found that formative assessment and the instructional decisions based on it can actually thwart the learning process. Assessment criteria were often about social and managerial aspects such as team work, like taking turns at the computer, rather than procedural and conceptual aspects of learning about computers.

Dassa (1990, p. 40) reminded readers that "an error is in practice defined as such essentially by the teacher. Hence errors express, at least partially, the type of relationship to knowledge that is gradually being built for the pupil." Consistent with Tunstall and Gipps's (1996) typology, Dassa's observation reminds us that we need to be careful about the criteria used in formative assessment, for they surely will "construct the way forward." It is important that pupils indeed go forward, not in some other direction, which will happen if the teachers' vision of the learning target is not what it should be.

Pupil Motivation

Motivational variables have been studied in relation to assessment in two ways, as both the independent variable (the effects of motivation on classroom learning) and as the dependent variable (the effects of classroom assessments on motivation). Most of the studies were essentially correlational in nature. No matter which way the prediction was run, the conclusions must remain that these variables are related, but the direction of causality is not clear. In fact, it may be a mutual cause and effect. Some variables that were identified as mediators in one study were predictors in others, too, so even the relationships among the causes are not clear.

A lot of work on achievement motivation has been done in classrooms. Blumenfeld (1992) summarized that research. Much of that work has used achievement goals themselves as the dependent variables of interest, but recently research in this field has begun to include classroom assessments as well.

Some of the studies reported earlier in this review included motivational variables. Several others have had motivation as the main focus. Brookhart and DeVoge (1999) concluded from pupil interviews that previous experience with similar assignments was the main source of information for self-efficacy judgments about current work. Pupils' general expectations about how they would do on assessments were based on perceptions of themselves as "good." Pupils' specific expectations were based on characteristics of particular assignments (e.g., "I always do well on spelling tests"). Alao and Guthrie (1999) found that prior knowledge predicted current conceptual understanding, as measured by a classroom test. Strategy use, interest, and learning goals were related; however, none of these alone was a significant predictor of conceptual understanding.

A few studies have hinted at differential motivational values for different types of assessments. Stefanou and Parkes (2003) investigated the effect of specific assessments on motivation. They pointed out that the benefits of using projects for assessment have been seen but rarely documented. They found a significant effect of assessment type on goal orientation in fifth-grade science: Paper-pencil tests and performance assessments both fostered more task-focused orientations than lab tests. Brookhart and Durkin (2003) theorized that performance assessment may stimulate pupils' desire for competence in both the absolute sense (mastery goal orientations) *and* the relative sense (performance goal orientations) at the same time. Meece and Miller (1999) did an intervention study in third-grade classrooms. They worked with teachers to encourage them to assign longer (multiday; requiring at least a paragraph response), more collaborative, and more thoughtful assignments. The third-grade pupils became less focused on performance goals and low-achieving pupils reported less work avoidance.

Turner, Thorpe, and Meyer (1998) found that different pupils have different motivational patterns. They identified four pupil patterns: learning-oriented, success-oriented, uncommitted, and avoidant. The existence of different patterns of pupil motivational approaches to learning has implications for classroom formative assessment. Unsuccessful pupils receive feedback while they are feeling badly after failure. Feedback must do something to deal with these negative feelings in order to break the cycle of failure; otherwise, the feedback will not serve to focus pupil attention on the work (Kluger & DeNisi, 1996).

If pupils are to reap the benefits of formative assessment, they must be able to use its information. Self-regulated learning involves pupils using metacognitive strategies (planning and monitoring their work and managing their effort). Self-regulated learning also involves pupils using cognitive strategies (rehearsal, elaboration, organization, engagement) in order to learn. Pintrich and DeGroot (1990) found that for seventh graders, self-regulation strategy use and cognitive strategy use related to performance on seatwork and on essays and reports. Formative feedback should teach pupils strategy use and then foster self-efficacy so the pupils will actually use the strategies. Cognitive strategies alone, without self-regulation, are not sufficient for achievement. "Pupils need to have both the 'will' and the 'skill' to be successful in classrooms" (Pintrich & DeGroot, 1990, p. 38). These findings about motivation are consistent with Kluger and DeNisi's (1996) theory that feedback serves to focus attention on performance at a level of abstraction about which pupils can do something.

They are also consistent with Ryan, Connell, and Deci's (1985) cognitive evaluation theory, which states that: 1) if an action results in the experience of autonomy or agency (an internal locus of control), it increases intrinsic motivation to act in that way; 2) if an action results in the perception of competence, it increases intrinsic motivation to act in that way; and 3) events vary in functional significance. The same events that result in feelings of competence one day may be perceived as externally imposed on another day. An event functions as informational if it leads to perceptions of competence; so, for example, feedback that a pupil finds really useful for improvement might be perceived as informational. An event functions as controlling if it does not lead to feelings of competence; so, for example, a simple grade on a paper might be perceived as controlling. Formative classroom assessment by definition must be informational.

Pupil Involvement in Assessment

Pupil involvement in their own assessment produces learning gains (Brookhart, Andolina, Zuza, & Furman, 2004). Two studies were found that addressed this directly (Ross, Hogaboam-Gray, & Rolheiser, 2002; Wiliam, Lee, Harrison, & Black, 2004). Additional evidence is provided by other studies of the effects of quality classroom assessment more generally. Further, it is a "short walk" from the motivation literature proper (from educational psychology) to this application.

There may be some developmental aspects to self-assessment. Ross, Rolheiser, and Hogaboam-Gray (2002) found that sixth graders were more thoughtful about evaluation information than younger pupils were. The sixth graders expressed less uncertainty and used more resources for interpretation, including more longitudinal comparisons. Younger pupils focused more on neatness and language. Higgins, Harris, and Kuehn (1994) found that even first graders could participate in generating their own criteria and assessing their own work, but pupils believed that the amount of work and cooperation was as important, if not more, than the product, and they believed that these skills should be graded.

Brookhart and Bronowicz (2003) also noticed a developmental progression. When asked what they were supposed to do for an assessment, pupils often described the mechanics of the assignment. Younger children also sometimes said they were simply supposed "to study." It seems there is at least a developmental progression in the ability to articulate what it means to succeed in school. Even within a developmental progression, pupil perceptions of and responses to assessments differ widely, as do the nature of pupils' journeys toward independence and self-evaluation (Klenoski, 1995; Moni, van Kraayenoord, & Baker, 2002).

Validity and Reliability

It seems that teachers are not knowledgeable about what measurement theorists would consider relevant reliability and validity principles (Campbell & Evans, 2000; Impara, Plake, & Fager, 1993; Mertler, 2000). Much more interesting are some studies of how assessments play out in classrooms that raise validity issues. One of these is a question raised by a teacher interviewed by Cizek, Fitzgerald, and Rachor (1995, p. 170): If different assessments are matters of teacher choice but are still intended to measure the same learning targets (curriculum goals and objectives), then among these interchangeable methods, isn't the particular choice of assessment ultimately irrelevant? I find this an interesting conundrum for validity theory, which, contrary to classroom practice, would suggest that the answer is no.

Two studies addressed validity by asking what particular tests and performance assessments were measuring. Parkes (2000) found that pupils' perceptions of control predicted performance on writing a paragraph in Spanish but not performance on a multiple-choice test of the same vocabulary. This raised the question of whether a "performance"-related motivational variable was construct-relevant or construct-irrelevant for this performance assessment. Nuthall and Alton-Lee (1995) asked pupils how they answered classroom test questions. They found that 30–50% of answers were recall of directly relevant information or classroom experiences; 15–24% of answers were arrived at by deducing answers from related experience and knowledge. Item-answering strategies were affected by the length of time (long-term, there was less direct recall and more deduction), the nature of the topic, pupil background knowledge, the type of learning experience, and involvement in classroom activities.

Bulterman-Bos, Terwel, Verloop, and Wardekker (2002) found that observation is embedded in the act of teaching. Teachers cannot separate themselves from the observations they make. The success of an observation (for example, supporting a productive or useful instructional decision) becomes a warrant for its validity. Several factors affect the validity of the information that teachers glean from their observations: 1) teachers differ in active observation, 2) the observation process is interpersonal, 3) teachers who observe play two roles simultaneously, 4) observation in teaching is a mutual influence process, 5) how results should be attributed is uncertain, 6) observation is never complete, and 7) images of former pupils play a role in discovering differences among current pupils.

Marzano (2002) studied the reliability of four different methods of scoring classroom assessments that required teacher judgment (i.e., not objective tests): unconstrained and constrained point methods, and general and task-specific rubrics. Not surprisingly, the more task-specific and constrained the method, the more reliable were teachers' judgments. Arter and McTighe (2001) argue that although task-specific rubrics are easier to use reliably at first, the instructional benefits of using generic rubrics are worth the extra time it takes to learn to use them—and to teach pupils to use them—reliably.

Effects of Formative Classroom Assessment on Pupil Achievement

Black and Wiliam (1998b) reported a typical effect size for studies of formative assessment on learning to be between 0.40 and 0.70. Six studies published since Black and Wiliam's (1998b) review investigated some aspect of the use of formative classroom assessment on learning and achievement. Where effect sizes are reported in these recent studies, they are mostly in the same general range reported by Black and Wiliam (1998b).

Two studies tested versions of my theory (Brookhart, 1997a) about the role of the classroom assessment environment in pupil achievement using large national databases. I (Brookhart, 1997b) found that math and science achievement was affected by several classroom assessment variables. Most of the classroom assessment environment variables that were significant predictors of achievement were teacher report variables, which "suggests that classroom controllables are important and that an environment can be created" (p. 328). Rodriguez (2004) found that self-efficacy and effort were related to achievement and were affected by classroom assessment practices. Self-efficacy had a stronger relative effect on achievement in classrooms where teachers did not use teacher-made objective tests heavily.

Ross, Hogaboam-Gray, and Rolheiser (2002) tested whether fifth- and sixth-grade pupils trained on how to do self-evaluation would have higher math achievement, as measured by a classroom performance task. Pupil self-evaluation was associated with higher math achievement, with an effect size of 0.40. The self-evaluation training included: 1) involving pupils in developing self-evaluation criteria, 2) teaching them how to apply the criteria, 3) giving pupils feedback on their self-evaluation, and 4) helping pupils use evaluation data to develop their action plans.

Three studies specifically investigated the question of whether using challenging intellectual work and formative assessment in the classroom would lead to achievement as measured by the external tests of educational outcomes often required currently. Interestingly, one was at the primary level (Meisels, Atkins-Burnett, Xue, & Bickel, 2003), one was at the elementary level (Newman, Bryk, & Nagaoka, 2001), and one was at the high school level (Wiliam, Lee, Harrison, & Black, 2004).

Meisels, Atkins-Burnett, Xue, and Bickel (2003) compared primary level children in Pittsburgh public schools who had used the Work Sampling System (WSS), a curriculum-embedded performance assessment system, for three years with non-WSS children in matched schools and with other children in the same school, on the Iowa Test of Basic Skills. In reading, the WSS group far outpaced the other two groups; the effect size was 0.68, compared with others in the same school, and 1.60 compared with matched pupils. In math, the effect size was 0.20 compared with others in the same school, and 0.76 compared with matched pupils. The difference for low achievers were greater in math than reading. The authors discussed the complementarity of performance-based and normative tests in accountability systems. They offered the explanation that multiple sources of information from WSS would lead to better instruction and would also lead pupils to become familiar with standards and how to progress toward them. With good performance-based formative assessment, the authors wrote: "'Will this be on the test?' ceases to be the question of learners. Instead, 'What should I learn next?' becomes the focus."

Wiliam, Lee, Harrison, and Black (2004) studied the impact on pupil achievement (defined as whatever outcome measure was used locally—for example, an external exam or a local science test) of teachers developing assessment for learning. They provided professional development about formative assessments for teachers, made visits to schools, and honored local designs for formative assessments. Effect sizes for different classes or different year pupils were calculated, using norms when available. Effect sizes were mostly 0.20 to 0.30, with a median of 0.27 and a mean of 0.34. The more experienced the teacher, the less spread out the effect sizes were. The authors interpreted their findings in light of how to support teachers in their practice, not about the effects of formative assessment *per se*. They noted that the formative assessment methods chosen were often traffic lights or smiley faces, combined almost always with instructions on how to follow up if the pupil did not understand. These simple methods fit the classroom culture and proved effective.

CONCLUSIONS

Formative assessment helps give pupils both the information they need to improve and the confidence and self-regulation they need to use it. Done well, it does not conflict with external measures of achievement. Formative assessment is the sleeping giant in classrooms. It's time to wake it up!

REFERENCES

Adams, T. L., & Hsu, J.W.Y. (1998). Classroom assessment: Teachers' conceptions and practices in mathematics. *School Science and Mathematics*, *98*, 174–180.

Alao, S., & Guthrie, J. T. (1999). Predicting conceptual understanding with cognitive and motivational variables. *Journal of Educational Research*, *92*, 243–254.

Arter, J., & McTighe, J. (2001). *Scoring rubrics in the classroom*. Thousand Oaks, CA: Corwin Press.

Bachor, D. G., & Baer, M. R. (2001). An examination of preservice teachers' simulated classroom assessment practices. *Alberta Journal of Educational Research*, *47*, 244–258.

Bangert-Drowns, R. L., Kulik, C. C., & Kulik, J. A. (1991). Effects of frequent classroom testing. *Journal of Educational Research*, *85*, 89–99.

Bangert-Drowns, R. L., Kulik, C. C., Kulik, J. A., & Morgan, M. (1991). The instructional effect of feedback in test-like events. *Review of Educational Research*, *61*, 213–238.

Barnes, S. (1985). A study of classroom pupil evaluation: The missing link in teacher education. *Journal of Teacher Education*, *36*(4), 46–49.

Biggs, J. (1998). Assessment and classroom learning: A role for summative assessment? *Assessment in Education*, *5*, 103–110.

Black, P., Harrison, C., Lee, C., Marshall, B., & Wiliam, D. (2004). Working inside the black box: Assessment for learning in the classroom. *Phi Delta Kappan*, *86*, 8–21.

Black, P., & Wiliam, D. (1998a). Assessment and classroom learning. *Assessment in Education*, *5*, 7–74.

Black, P., & Wiliam, D. (1998b). Inside the black box: Raising standards through classroom assessment. *Phi Delta Kappan*, *80*, 139–144.

Bloom, B. (1984). The search for methods of group instruction as effective as one-to-one tutoring. *Educational Leadership*, *41*(8), 4–17.

Bloom, B. S., Hastings, J. T., & Madaus, G. F. (1971). *Handbook on formative and summative evaluation of pupil learning*. New York: McGraw-Hill.

Blumenfeld, P. C. (1992). Classroom learning and motivation: Clarifying and expanding goal theory. *Journal of Educational Psychology*, *84*, 272–281.

Brookhart, S. M. (1997a). A theoretical framework for the role of classroom assessment in motivating pupil effort and achievement. *Applied Measurement in Education*, *10*, 161–180.

Brookhart, S. M. (1997b). Effects of the classroom assessment environment on mathematics and science achievement. *Journal of Educational Research, 90,* 323–330.

Brookhart, S. M. (2001). Successful pupils' formative and summative uses of assessment information. *Assessment in Education, 8,* 153–169.

Brookhart, S. M. (2003). Developing measurement theory for classroom assessment purposes and uses. *Educational Measurement: Issues and Practice, 22,* 5–12.

Brookhart, S. M. (2004). Classroom assessment: Tensions and intersections in theory and practice. *Teachers College Record, 106,* 429–458.

Brookhart, S. M., Andolina, M., Zuza, M., & Furman, R. (2004). Minute math: An action research study of pupil self-assessment. *Educational Studies in Mathematics, 57,* 213–227.

Brookhart, S. M., & Bronowicz, D. L. (2003). "I don't like writing. It makes my fingers hurt": Pupils talk about their classroom assessments. *Assessment in Education, 10,* 221–242.

Brookhart, S. M., & DeVoge, J. G. (1999). Testing a theory about the role of classroom assessment in pupil motivation and achievement. *Applied Measurement in Education, 12,* 409–425.

Brookhart, S. M., & Durkin, D. T. (2003). Classroom assessment, pupil motivation, and achievement in high school social studies. *Applied Measurement in Education, 16,* 27–54.

Brown, G.T.L. (2004). Teachers' conceptions of assessment: Implications for policy and professional development. *Assessment in Education, 11,* 301–318.

Bulterman-Bos, J., Terwel, J., Verloop, N., & Wardekker, W. (2002). Observation in teaching: Toward a practice of objectivity. *Teachers College Record, 104,* 1069–1100.

Butler, R. (1987). Task-involving and ego-involving properties of evaluation: Effects of different feedback conditions on motivational perceptions, interest, and performance. *Journal of Educational Psychology, 79,* 474–482.

Butler, R., & Nisan, M. (1986). Effects of no feedback, task-related comments, and grades on intrinsic motivation and performance. *Journal of Educational Psychology, 78,* 210–216.

Campbell, C., & Evans, J. A. (2000). Investigation of preservice teachers' classroom assessment practices during pupil teaching. *Journal of Educational Research, 93,* 350–355.

Church, M. A., Elliot, A. J., & Gable, S. L. (2001). Perceptions of classroom environment, achievement goals, and achievement outcomes. *Journal of Educational Psychology, 93,* 43–54.

Cicmanec, K. M., & Viechnicki, K. J. (1994). Assessing mathematics skills through portfolios: Validating the claims from existing literature. *Educational Assessment, 2,* 167–178.

Cizek, G. J., Fitzgerald, S. M., & Rachor, R. E. (1995). Teachers' assessment practices: Preparation, isolation, and the kitchen sink. *Educational Assessment, 3,* 159–179.

Crooks, T. J. (1988). The impact of classroom evaluation practices on pupils. *Review of Educational Research, 58,* 438–481.

Dassa, C. (1990). From a horizontal to a vertical method of integrating educational diagnosis with classroom assessment. *Alberta Journal of Educational Research, 36*, 35–44.

Elawar, M. C., & Corno, L. (1985). A factorial experiment in teachers' written feedback on pupil homework: Changing teacher behavior a little rather than a lot. *Journal of Educational Psychology, 77*, 162–173.

Frary, R. B., Cross, L. H., & Weber, L. J. (1993). Testing and grading practices and opinions of secondary teachers of academic subjects: Implications for instruction in measurement. *Educational Measurement: Issues and Practice, 12*(3), 23–30.

Frisbie, D. A., Miranda, D. U., & Baker, K. K. (1993). An evaluation of elementary textbook tests as classroom assessment tools. *Applied Measurement in Education, 6*, 21–36.

Gipps, C., McCallum, B., & Hargreaves, E. (2000). *What makes a good primary school teacher? Expert classroom strategies*. London: Routledge Falmer.

Goldberg, G. L., & Roswell, B. S. (1999–2000). From perception to practice: The impact of teachers' scoring experience on performance-based instruction and classroom assessment. *Educational Assessment, 6*, 257–290.

Gullickson, A. R. (1985). Pupil evaluation techniques and their relationship to grade and curriculum. *Journal of Educational Research, 79*, 96–100.

Higgins, K. M., Harris, N. A., & Kuehn, L. L. (1994). Placing assessment into the hands of young children: A study of self-generated criteria and self-assessment. *Educational Assessment, 2*, 309–324.

Impara, J. C., Plake, B. S., & Fager, J. J. (1993). Educational administrators' and teachers' knowledge of classroom assessment. *Journal of School Leadership, 3*, 510–521.

Isaacson, S. (1999). Instructionally relevant writing assessment. *Reading and Writing Quarterly: Overcoming Learning Difficulties, 15*, 29–48.

Johnson, S. T., Wallace, M. B., & Thompson, S. D. (1999). Broadening the scope of assessment in schools: Building teacher efficacy in pupil assessment. *Journal of Negro Education, 68*, 397–408.

Kahn, E. A. (2000). A case study of assessment in a grade 10 English course. *Journal of Educational Research, 93*, 276–286.

Klenowski, V. (1995). Pupil self-evaluation processes in pupil-centered teaching and learning contexts of Australia and England. *Assessment in Education, 2*, 145–163.

Kluger, A. N., & DeNisi, A. (1996). The effects of feedback interventions on performance: A historical review, a meta-analysis, and a preliminary feedback intervention theory. *Psychological Bulletin, 119*, 254–284.

Kusch, J. W. (1999). The dimensions of classroom assessment: How field study pupils learn to grade in the middle level classroom. *Journal of Educational Thought (Revue de la Pensee Educative), 33*(1), 61–81.

Marzano, R. J. (2002). A comparison of selected methods of scoring classroom assessments. *Applied Measurement in Education, 15*, 249–267.

Mavrommatis, Y. (1997). Understanding assessment in the classroom: Phases of the assessment process—the assessment episode. *Assessment in Education, 4*, 381–400.

McMillan, J. H. (2001). Secondary teachers' classroom assessment and grading practices. *Educational Measurement: Issues and Practice, 20*(1), 20–32.

McMillan, J. H. (2003). Understanding and improving teachers' classroom assessment decision making. *Educational Measurement: Issues and Practice, 22*(4), 34–43.

McMillan, J. H., Myran, S., & Workman, D. (2002). Elementary teachers' classroom assessment and grading practices. *Journal of Educational Research, 95*, 203–213.

Meece, J. L., & Miller, S. D. (1999). Changes in elementary school children's achievement goals for reading and writing: Results of a longitudinal and an intervention study. *Scientific Studies of Reading, 3*, 207–229.

Meisels, S., Atkins-Burnett, S., Xue, Y., & Bickel, D. D. (2003). Creating a system of accountability: The impact of instructional assessment on elementary children's achievement scores. *Educational Policy Analysis Archives, 11*(9). Retrieved April 2006, from http://epaa.asu.edu/eapp/v11n9/

Mertler, C. A. (2000). Teacher-centered fallacies of classroom assessment validity and reliability. *Mid-Western Educational Researcher, 13*(4), 29–35.

Moni, K. B., van Kraayenoord, C. E., & Baker, C. D. (2002). Pupils' perceptions of literacy assessment. *Assessment in Education, 9*, 319–342.

Moreland, J., & Jones, A. (2000). Emerging assessment practices in an emergent curriculum: Implications for technology. *International Journal of Technology and Design Education, 10*, 283–305.

Natriello, G. (1987). The impact of evaluation processes on pupils. *Educational Psychologist, 22*, 155–175.

Natriello, G. (1996). Evaluation processes and pupil disengagement from high school. In A. M. Pallas (Ed.), *Research in sociology of education and socialization* (*Vol. 11*, pp. 147–172). Greenwich, CT: JAI Press.

Newmann, F. M., Bryk, A. S., & Nagaoka, J. K. (2001, January). *Authentic intellectual work and standardized tests: Conflict or coexistence?* Chicago: Consortium on Chicago School Research.

Nicholson, D. J., & Anderson, J. O. (1993). A time and place for observations: Talking with primary teachers about classroom assessment. *Alberta Journal of Educational Research, 39*, 363–374.

Niemi, D. (1997). Cognitive science, expert-novice research, and performance assessment. *Theory into Practice, 36*, 239–246.

Nuthall, G., & Alton-Lee, A. (1995). Assessing classroom learning: How pupils use their knowledge and experience to answer classroom achievement test questions in science and social studies. *American Educational Research Journal, 32*, 185–223.

Parkes, J. (2000). The interaction of assessment format and examinees' perceptions of control. *Educational Research, 42*, 175–182.

Pintrich, P. R., & DeGroot, E. V. (1990). Motivational and self-regulated learning components of classroom academic performance. *Journal of Educational Psychology, 82*, 33–40.

Pryor, J., & Akwesi, C. (1998). Assessment in Ghana and England: Putting reform to the test of practice. *Compare, 28*, 263–275.

Raveaud, M. (2004). Assessment in French and English infant schools: Assessing the work, the child, or the culture? *Assessment in Education, 11,* 193–211.

Rea-Dickens, P. (2001). Mirror, mirror on the wall: Identifying the processes of classroom assessment. *Language Testing, 18,* 429–462.

Rodriguez, M. C. (2004). The role of classroom assessment in pupil performance on TIMMS. *Applied Measurement in Education, 17,* 1–24.

Rosenholtz, S. J., & Rosenholtz, S. H. (1981). Classroom organization and the perception of ability. *Sociology of Education, 54,* 132–140.

Ross, J. A., Hogaboam-Gray, A., & Rolheiser, C. (2002). Pupil self-evaluation in grade 5–6 mathematics: Effects on problem-solving achievement. *Educational Assessment, 8,* 43–58.

Ross, J. A., Rolheiser, C., & Hogaboam-Gray, A. (2002). Influences on pupil cognitions about evaluation. *Assessment in Education, 9,* 81–95.

Ryan, R. M., Connell, J. P., & Deci, E. L. (1985). A motivational analysis of self-determination and self-regulation in the classroom. In C. Ames and R. Ames (Eds.), *Research on motivation in education: Vol. 2. The classroom milieu* (pp. 13–51). Orlando, FL: Academic.

Sadler, D. R. (1983). Evaluation and the improvement of academic learning. *Journal of Higher Education, 54,* 60–79.

Sadler, D. R. (1989). Formative assessment and the design of instructional systems. *Instructional Science, 18,* 119–144.

Schmidt, M. E., & Brosnan, P. A. (1996). Mathematics assessment: Practices and reporting methods. *School Science and Mathematics, 96,* 17–20.

Scriven, M. (1967). The methodology of evaluation. In R. W. Tyler, R. M. Gagne, & M. Scriven (Eds.), *Perspectives of curriculum evaluation.* Chicago: Rand McNally.

Shepard, L. A. (2001). The role of classroom assessment in teaching and learning. In V. Richardson (Ed.), *Handbook of research on teaching* (4th ed., pp. 1066–1101). Washington, DC: AERA.

Simpson, C. (1981). Classroom structure and the organization of ability. *Sociology of Education, 54,* 120–132.

Stefanou, C., & Parkes, J. (2003). Effects of classroom assessment on pupil motivation in fifth-grade science. *Journal of Educational Research, 96,* 152–162.

Stiggins, R. J. (1999). Assessment, pupil confidence, and school success. *Phi Delta Kappan, 81,* 191–198.

Stiggins, R. J. (2005). *Pupil-involved assessment FOR learning* (4th ed.). Upper Saddle River, NJ: Pearson Merrill Prentice Hall.

Stiggins, R. J., & Bridgeford, N. J. (1985). The ecology of classroom assessment. *Journal of Educational Measurement, 22,* 271–286.

Stiggins, R. J., & Conklin, N. F. (1992). *In teachers' hands: Investigating the practices of classroom assessment.* Albany, NY: SUNY Press.

Stiggins, R. J., Griswold, M. M., & Wikelund, K. R. (1989). Measuring thinking skills through classroom assessment. *Journal of Educational Measurement, 26,* 233–246.

Thomas, S., & Oldfather, P. (1997). Intrinsic motivations, literacy, and assessment practices: "That's my grade. That's me." *Educational Psychologist, 32,* 107–123.

Tittle, C. K. (1994). Toward an educational psychology of assessment for teaching and learning: Theories, contexts, and validation arguments. *Educational Psychologist, 29,* 149–162.

Torrance, H., & Pryor, J. (1998). *Investigating formative assessment.* Buckingham, UK: Open University Press.

Torrance, H., & Pryor, J. (2001). Developing formative assessment in the classroom: Using action research to explore and modify theory. *British Educational Research Journal, 27,* 615–631.

Traub, R. E. (1990). Assessment in the classroom: What is the role of research? *Alberta Journal of Educational Research, 36*(1), 85–91.

Tunstall, P., & Gipps, C. (1996). Teacher feedback to young children in formative assessment: A typology. *British Educational Research Journal, 22,* 389–404.

Turner, J. C., Thorpe, P. K., & Meyer, D. K. (1998). Pupils' reports of motivation and negative affect: A theoretical and empirical analysis. *Journal of Educational Psychology, 90,* 758–771.

Wiliam, D., & Black, P. J. (1996). Meanings and consequences: A basis for distinguishing formative and summative functions of assessment? *British Educational Research Journal, 22,* 537–548.

Wiliam, D., Lee, C., Harrison, C., & Black, P. (2004). Teachers developing assessment for learning: Impact on pupil achievement. *Assessment in Education, 11,* 49–65.

Wilson, R. J. (1990). Classroom processes in evaluating pupil achievement. *Alberta Journal of Educational Research, 36,* 4–17.

Wolf, D. P. (1993). Assessment as an episode of learning. In R. E. Bennet & W. C. Ward (Eds.), *Construction versus choice in cognitive measurement* (pp. 213–240). Hillsdale, NJ: Lawrence Erlbaum.

Zhang, Z., & Burry-Stock, J. A. (2003). Classroom assessment practices and teachers' self-perceived assessment skills. *Applied Measurement in Education, 16,* 323–342.

CHAPTER 5

Formative Classroom Assessment and Benjamin S. Bloom: Theory, Research, and Practice

Thomas R. Guskey

Achievement gaps among different groups of pupils in American schools have been evident for many years. In the 1960s, President Lyndon Johnson's "War on Poverty" focused directly on identified inequalities in the educational achievement of economically disadvantaged pupils and their more advantaged counterparts. The Economic Opportunity Act (EOA) of 1964, which established the Head Start program, and the Elementary and Secondary Education Act (ESEA) of 1965, which created the Title I and Follow-Through programs, were specific attempts to address these disparities in educational attainment.

In recent years, achievement gaps have attracted renewed attention from policy makers and legislators. Recognizing that a highly skilled workforce is essential for success in today's global economy, public officials have enacted new legislation that requires educators to ensure that *all* pupils achieve at high levels. These new laws compel school leaders to report pupil achievement results separately for various poverty, ethnicity, language, and disability subgroups. Not only must they identify any achievement gaps among these different subgroups, but they also must take specific steps to close them.

Educational researchers have studied achievement differences extensively over the years and have learned a great deal about what works and what does not work in reducing them. Modern proposals for closing achievement gaps, however, frequently ignore this important knowledge base. As a result, many simply "reinvent" well-established principles while others seem destined to repeat past errors, waste valuable resources, and frustrate policy makers and practitioners alike.

To succeed in our efforts to close achievement gaps and reach the goal of helping *all* pupils learn well, we must build on and extend this hard-earned knowledge base. We must apply what we know in the context of modern classrooms and schools, add to our knowledge about what works, and then use that new knowledge to improve our effectiveness even more.

This chapter describes the work of one of the foremost contributors to our current knowledge base: Benjamin S. Bloom. We will consider how Bloom conceptualized and addressed the problem of achievement gaps, as well as the success that he and his pupils achieved in reducing achievement gaps through the use of mastery learning. We will describe the essential elements of mastery learning, especially its use of formative classroom assessments; discuss common misinterpretations; and conclude with a summary of the research on its effects in various school contexts.

THE CONTRIBUTION OF BENJAMIN S. BLOOM

When researchers study a problem, they try to reduce it to its simplest and most basic form. Educational researchers who study pupil learning, for example, tend to view achievement gaps simply as a matter of "variation": Pupils vary in their levels of achievement. Some pupils learn excellently in school and reach high levels of achievement, while others learn less well and attain only modest levels. Whenever we measure the achievement of two or more pupils, we also measure this "variation."

The purpose of most research studies is to "explain" variation. Researchers make educated guesses, called "hypotheses," about what factors contribute to identified differences among individuals or groups. They then manipulate those factors in carefully planned investigations to determine the effects. When they find a relationship between the factors that they manipulate and differences in the outcomes, they succeed in "explaining" variation.

One of the early researchers concerned with explaining variation in pupil learning was Benjamin S. Bloom (see Guskey, 2006). In the early 1960s, Bloom initiated a series of studies on individual differences, especially in school achievement. Although he recognized that numerous factors outside of school affect how well children learn, Bloom believed that educators potentially have strong influence as well (Bloom, 1964).

To determine the extent of educators' influence, Bloom began by observing teachers at a variety of grade levels in different schools. He discovered across these varied contexts that the majority of teachers taught all of their pupils in much the same way and provided all pupils with the same amount of time to learn. In other words, there was relatively little variation in each teacher's teaching. Pupils for whom these instructional methods and time were ideal learned excellently. The largest number of pupils found these methods and time only moderately appropriate and learned less well. Pupils for whom the instruction and time were inappropriate, due to differences in their backgrounds or learning styles, typically learned very little. In other words, *little* variation in the teaching resulted in *great* variation in pupil learning.

To attain better results and reduce this variation in pupil achievement, Bloom reasoned that we would have to increase variation in the teaching. That is, because pupils vary in their learning styles and aptitudes, we must diversify and differentiate instruction to better meet their individual learning needs. The challenge was to find practical ways to do this within the constraints of group-based classrooms so that *all* pupils learn well.

In searching for such a strategy, Bloom drew primarily from two sources of evidence. First, he considered the ideal teaching and learning situation in which an excellent tutor is paired with each pupil. He was particularly influenced by the work of early pioneers in individualized instruction, especially Washburne (1922) and his Winnetka Plan, and Morrison (1926) and his University of Chicago Laboratory School experiments. In examining this evidence, Bloom tried to determine which critical elements in one-to-one tutoring and individualized instruction could be transferred to group-based classroom settings.

Second, Bloom looked at studies of the learning strategies of academically successful pupils. From this research, he tried to identify the activities of high-achieving pupils in group-based classrooms that distinguish them from their less successful classmates.

To Bloom, it seemed reasonable for teachers to organize the concepts and skills they wanted pupils to learn into instructional units and then to teach those units as they thought best. He also considered it valuable for teachers to assess pupil learning at the end of each unit. However, he found that most teachers' classroom assessments did little more than show the pupils for whom their initial instruction was and was not appropriate. These assessments served solely as evaluation devices, used by teachers mainly to determine pupils' grades.

A far better approach, according to Bloom, would be for teachers to use their classroom assessments as an integral part of the instructional process. Doing so, however, would require three major changes. Specifically, teachers needed to 1) view their classroom assessments primarily as sources of information, 2) follow their assessments with high-quality corrective instruction, and 3) give pupils a second chance on assessments to show improvement and to demonstrate success.

Classroom Assessments as Sources of Information

Bloom found that a common experience for pupils was to spend time and energy preparing for a classroom assessment only to discover that the material or concepts they had studied were different from what the teacher emphasized on the assessment. This experience teaches pupils that hard work and effort often do not pay off in school. It also convinces many pupils that teachers cannot be trusted (Guskey, 2000). These hardly seem to be the lessons that responsible teachers want their pupils to learn.

This experience stems from the long-held but mistaken belief that assessments must be kept secret and that it is unfair to let pupils know what will be included on an assessment. Sadly, this also leads many pupils to regard assessments as guessing games. As a result, they come to believe that their success in school depends largely on how well they can guess what their teachers will ask on quizzes, tests, and other types of assessments.

Bloom recommended that teachers use their classroom assessments instead as sources of information, or "feedback," for pupils. Rather than surprising pupils, classroom assessments should be well-aligned with the teachers' instructional activities and should inform pupils about what they have achieved. To emphasize this "informing" purpose, Bloom (1968) recommended calling them "formative" assessments, borrowing the term from Scriven (1967), who used it a year earlier to describe the informative, rather than judgmental, aspects of program evaluations.

Bloom stressed that formative classroom assessments should reflect the specific concepts and skills the teacher had emphasized in class, along with the criteria that the teacher taught for judging pupils' performance. He further stressed that they should facilitate pupils' learning by providing pupils with essential feedback on their learning progress. They should help pupils recognize their learning successes, but also help them identify any learning problems (Bloom, Hastings, & Madaus, 1971; Stiggins, 2002).

In addition, Bloom emphasized that formative classroom assessments should serve as meaningful sources of information and "feedback" for teachers as well. They should help teachers identify what was taught well and what areas need refinement or revision. As such, formative assessments provide teachers with specific guidance in their efforts to improve the quality of their teaching (Guskey, 1987).

High-Quality, Corrective Instruction

If classroom assessments serve as a source of information for both pupils and teachers, it naturally followed for Bloom that these assessments cannot mark the end of learning. Instead, formative classroom assessments must be followed by high-quality, corrective instruction designed to help pupils remedy whatever learning errors were identified on the assessment (see Guskey, 1997.

To charge ahead knowing that certain concepts or skills have not been learned well seemed particularly foolish to Bloom. He recommended instead that teachers follow their formative classroom assessments with instructional alternatives that present the unit concepts or skills differently and engage pupils in different, and more appropriate, learning experiences.

Bloom emphasized, however, that high-quality, corrective instruction is not the same as reteaching, which typically involves restating original explanations louder and more slowly. Rather, it requires the use of instructional approaches that accommodate differences in pupils' learning styles, modalities, and forms of intelligence (Sternberg, 1994). Although teachers generally consider some of these differences when they initially plan their lessons, Bloom's idea was that corrective instruction must extend and strengthen that work. He also emphasized that pupils who perform well on the formative assessment and have few or no learning errors to correct should be offered high-quality enrichment or extension activities that give them the opportunity to broaden and expand their learning.

Teachers sometimes express concern that taking time to offer this corrective instruction will limit curriculum coverage. In other words, they believe they will have to reduce the number of concepts or skills that they present. Bloom stressed, however, that this need not be the case.

Because corrective work initially must be done in class, under the teacher's direction, early instructional units may require more time, perhaps an extra class period or two. But as pupils become accustomed to this process and realize the personal benefits it offers, Bloom recommended that the amount of class time allocated to corrective work be reduced. More could be handled through homework assignments or in special study sessions before or after school. In addition, when minor errors are not permitted to become major learning problems, pupils are better prepared for subsequent learning tasks and require less time for corrective work (Whiting, Van Burgh, & Render, 1995). For this reason, instruction in later learning units can proceed at a more rapid pace. As a result, Bloom believed that teachers need not sacrifice curriculum coverage to offer pupils the benefits of high-quality corrective instruction, although they will need to be more flexible in pacing their instructional units.

Opportunities to Show Improvement and Demonstrate Success

To become an integral part of the instructional process, classroom assessments cannot be a "one-shot, do-or-die" experience for pupils. Instead, Bloom stressed that assessments must become a vital component in an ongoing effort to help pupils learn. If assessments are followed by high-quality corrective instruction designed to help pupils remedy their learning errors, then pupils must be given a second chance to demonstrate their new level of competence and understanding. Bloom pointed out that this "second chance" not only provides a means for determining the effectiveness of the corrective instruction, but it also gives pupils another opportunity to experience success in learning. Hence, it has great motivational power.

Writing teachers have long recognized the many benefits of a second chance. They know that pupils rarely write well on an initial attempt. Therefore, they build into the writing process opportunities for pupils to gain feedback on early writing drafts and then use that feedback to revise and improve their compositions and other writing samples. Bloom found that teachers of other subjects frequently balk at the idea, however, mainly because it differs from their personal learning experiences.

Some teachers express concern about the fairness of giving pupils a "second chance" and point out that "Life is not like that." They describe how a surgeon does not get a second chance to perform an operation successfully. Likewise, a pilot does not get a second chance to land a jumbo jet safely. Because of the very high stakes involved, each is required to get it right the first time.

What must be remembered in each of these cases, however, is how these highly skilled professionals were trained. The first operation performed by that surgeon was on a cadaver—a dead person. This clearly allows a lot of latitude for mistakes. Similarly, the pilot was required to spend many hours in a flight simulator before ever attempting a landing from the cockpit. In both of these instances, mistakes are recognized as an inherent part of the learning process. Such experiences allowed these professionals to learn from their mistakes and improve their performance. Similar training techniques are used in nearly every professional endeavor. Only in schools do pupils face the prospects of "one shot, do-or-die," with no chance to demonstrate what they learned from previous mistakes.

Furthermore, Bloom pointed out that all educators strive to have their pupils become "lifelong learners," and to develop "learning-to-learn" skills. What better learning-to-learn skill is there than the idea that you learn from your mistakes? All teachers want their pupils to recognize that a mistake does not mean learning is over. Perhaps it is just beginning. Some modern assessment experts argue, in fact, that pupils learn nothing from a successful performance. They only learn when that performance is less than successful, for then they can gain guidance and direction on how to improve (Wiggins, 1998).

BLOOM'S MASTERY LEARNING

Benjamin Bloom outlined a specific instructional strategy to make use of these changes, specifically the feedback, corrective, and second-chance elements, labeling it "learning for mastery" (Bloom, 1968), and later shortening the name to simply "mastery learning" (Bloom, 1974). With this strategy, teachers first organize the concepts and skills they want pupils to learn into instructional units that typically involve about a week or two of instructional time. Following initial instruction on the unit, teachers administer a brief assessment based on the unit's learning goals. Instead of signifying the end of the unit, this formative assessment's purpose is to give both pupils and teacher information, or "feedback," on each pupil's learning progress. It helps pupils and teachers identify specifically what has been learned well to that point and what has not (Bloom, Hastings, & Madaus, 1971).

Paired with each formative assessment are specific "corrective" activities for pupils to use in remedying their learning difficulties. Most teachers match these "correctives" to each item or set of prompts within the assessment so that pupils only need to work on those concepts or skills they have not yet mastered. In other words, the correctives are "individualized." They may point out additional sources of information on a particular topic, such as page numbers in the textbook or workbook where the topic is discussed. They may identify alternative learning resources such as different textbooks, learning kits, alternative materials, CDs, videos, or computerized instructional lessons. Or they may simply suggest sources of additional practice, such as study guides, independent or guided practice activities, or collaborative group activities. In most classrooms, teachers direct the corrective activities, but in some, pupils work independently or in small groups.

With the feedback and corrective information gained from a formative assessment, each pupil has a detailed prescription of what more needs to be done in order to master the concepts or skills from the unit. This "just-in-time" correction prevents minor learning difficulties from accumulating and becoming major learning problems. It also gives teachers a practical means to vary and differentiate their instruction in order to better meet pupils' individual learning needs. As a result, many more pupils learn well, master the important learning goals in each unit, and gain the necessary prerequisites for success in subsequent units.

When pupils complete their corrective activities after a class period or two, Bloom recommended they take a *second* formative assessment. This second, "parallel" assessment covers the same concepts and skills as the first, but is composed of slightly different problems or questions and serves two important purposes. First, it verifies whether or not the correctives were successful in helping pupils overcome their individual learning difficulties. Second, it offers pupils a second chance at success, thus providing powerful motivation.

Some pupils, of course, will perform well on the first assessment, demonstrating that they have mastered the unit concepts and skills. The teacher's initial instruction was highly appropriate for these pupils and they have no need of corrective work. To ensure their continued learning progress, Bloom recommended that these pupils be provided with special enrichment or extension activities to broaden their learning experiences. Such activities often are self-selected by pupils and might involve special projects or reports, academic games, or a variety of complex, problem-solving tasks. Materials designed for gifted and talented pupils provide an excellent source of enrichment or extension activities. Figure 5.1 illustrates this instructional sequence.

Through this process of formative classroom assessment, combined with the systematic correction of individual learning difficulties, Bloom believed all pupils could be provided with a more appropriate quality of instruction than is possible under more traditional approaches to teaching. As a result, nearly all pupils might be expected to learn well and truly master the unit concepts or learning goals (Bloom, 1976). This, in turn, would drastically reduce the variation in pupils' achievement levels, eliminate achievement gaps, and yield a distribution of achievement similar to that shown in Figure 5.2.

In describing mastery learning, however, Bloom emphasized that reducing variation in pupils' achievement does not imply making all pupils the same. Even under these more favorable learning conditions, some pupils undoubtedly will learn more than others, especially those who are involved in enrichment activities. But by recognizing relevant, individual differences among pupils and then altering instruction to better meet their diverse learning needs, Bloom believed that the variation among pupils in terms of how well they learn specific concepts or master a set of articulated learning goals could eventually reach a "vanishing point" (Bloom, 1973). As a result, gaps in the achievement of different groups of pupils would be closed and all pupils could be helped to learn excellently.

ESSENTIAL ELEMENTS OF MASTERY LEARNING

After Benjamin Bloom presented his ideas on mastery learning, others described procedures for implementation and numerous programs based on

Figure 5.1. The Mastery Learning Instructional Process

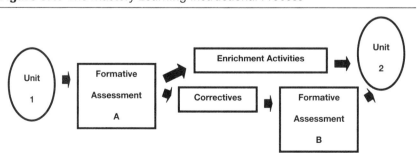

Figure 5.2. Distribution of Achievement in Mastery Learning Classrooms

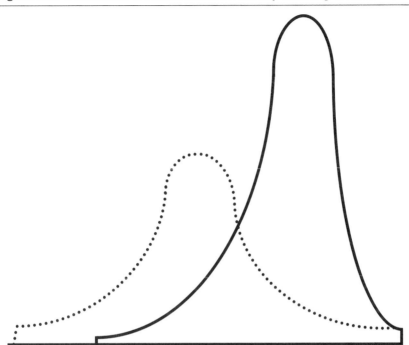

mastery learning principles sprung up in schools and colleges throughout the United States and around the world (e.g., Block, 1971, 1974; Block & Anderson, 1975). Although these programs differed from setting to setting, those that held true to Bloom's ideas included two essential elements: 1) the feedback, corrective, and enrichment process, and 2) instructional alignment (Guskey, 1997).

Feedback, Correctives, and Enrichment

Teachers who use mastery learning provide pupils with frequent and specific feedback on their learning progress through the use of regular, formative classroom assessments. Furthermore, this feedback is both diagnostic and prescriptive. It reinforces precisely what the teacher expected pupils to learn, identifies what was learned well, and describes what needs to be learned better. The National Council of Teachers of Mathematics (NCTM) emphasizes this same element in its latest iteration of standards for school mathematics. To overcome inequities in mathematics instruction, NCTM stresses the use of assessments that support learning and provide useful information to both teachers and pupils (National Council of Teachers of Mathematics, 2000).

Feedback alone, however, does little to help pupils improve their learning. Significant improvement requires the feedback be paired with correctives: activities that offer guidance and direction to pupils on how to remedy their learning problems. Because of pupils' individual differences, no single method of instruction works well for all of them. To help every pupil learn well, therefore, teachers must differentiate their instruction, both in their initial teaching and especially through corrective activities (Bloom, 1976). In other words, teachers must *increase* variation in their teaching in order to *decrease* variation in results.

To be optimally effective, correctives must be qualitatively different from the initial teaching. They must provide pupils who need it with an alternative approach and additional time to learn. The best correctives present concepts differently and involve pupils in learning in ways that are different from the teacher's initial instruction. They incorporate different learning styles, learning modalities, or types of intelligence. Although developing effective correctives can prove challenging, many schools find that providing teachers with time to work collaboratively so they can share ideas, materials, and expertise greatly facilitates the process (Guskey, 2001).

In most applications of mastery learning, correctives are accompanied by enrichment or extension activities for pupils who master the unit concepts from the initial teaching. As described above, enrichment activities offer pupils exciting opportunities to broaden and expand their learning. They reward pupils for their learning success but also challenge them to go further. Many teachers draw from activities developed for gifted and talented pupils when planning enrichment activities, both to simplify implementation tasks and to guarantee pupils a high-quality learning experience.

Teachers implement the feedback, corrective, and enrichment process in a variety of ways. Many use short, paper-and-pencil quizzes as formative assessments to give pupils feedback on their learning progress. However, formative assessments also can take the form of essays, and other compositions, projects, reports, performance tasks, skill demonstrations, oral presentations, or any means used to gain evidence of pupils' learning progress.

Following a formative assessment, some teachers divide the class into separate corrective and enrichment groups. While the teacher directs corrective activities, guaranteeing that all pupils with learning difficulties take part, the other pupils work on self-selected, independent enrichment activities. Other teachers pair with colleagues and use a team-teaching approach. While one teacher oversees corrective activities, the other monitors enrichments. Still other teachers use cooperative learning activities in which pupils work together in teams to ensure that they all reach the mastery level (Johnson,

Johnson, & Holubec, 1994). If all pupils attain mastery on the second formative assessment, the entire team receives special recognition or credit.

Feedback, corrective, and enrichment procedures are crucial to mastery learning, because it is through these procedures that mastery learning differentiates and individualizes instruction. In every unit taught, pupils who need extended time and opportunity to remedy learning problems are offered these through correctives. Those pupils who learn quickly and for whom the initial instruction was highly appropriate are provided with opportunities to extend their learning through enrichment. As a result, all pupils are provided with more favorable learning conditions and more appropriate, higher-quality instruction (Bloom, 1977).

Instructional Alignment

Although feedback, correctives, and enrichment are extremely important, they alone do not constitute mastery learning. To be truly effective, Bloom stressed that these techniques must be combined with the second essential element of mastery learning: instructional alignment.

Most educators see the teaching and learning process as having three major components. First, there must be some idea about what we want pupils to learn and be able to do; that is, learning goals or standards (see Stiggins, Chapter 2). This is followed by instruction that, hopefully, results in competent learners—pupils who have learned well and whose competence or proficiency can be determined through some form of assessment or evaluation. Mastery learning adds the feedback and corrective component in which teachers use formative classroom assessments to determine for which pupils their initial instruction was appropriate and for which learning alternatives may be needed.

Although essentially neutral with regard to what is taught, how it is taught, and how learning is assessed or evaluated, mastery learning requires consistency or alignment among these instructional components, as shown in Figure 5.3. If, for example, pupils are expected to learn higher-level skills such as those involved in making applications, problem solving, or analysis, mastery learning stipulates that instructional activities must be planned to give pupils opportunities to practice and actively engage in those skills. It also requires that pupils be given specific feedback on how well they have learned those skills, coupled with directions on how to correct any learning errors. Finally, procedures for evaluating pupils' learning should reflect those higher-level skills as well.

Ensuring alignment among instructional components requires teachers to make several crucial decisions. They must decide, for example, which concepts or skills are most important for pupils to learn and which are most central to pupils' understanding. They also must decide what evidence best reflects pupils' mastery of those concepts or skills, since this will determine

Figure 5.3. Major Components in the Teaching and Learning Process

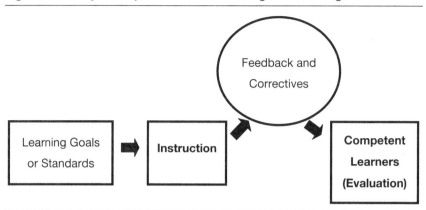

the type of the formative assessments they use. However, in essence, teachers at all levels make these decisions already. Every time they administer an assessment, grade a paper, or evaluate pupils' learning, teachers communicate to pupils what they consider to be most important. Using mastery learning simply compels teachers to make these decisions more thoughtfully and intentionally (see Guskey, 2005).

Studies show mastery learning to be particularly effective when applied to instruction that focuses on higher-level learning goals, such as problem solving, drawing inferences, deductive reasoning, and creative expression (Guskey, 1997). The process helps teachers close achievement gaps in a broad range of learning goals from basic knowledge and skills to highly complex cognitive processes.

When they first consider mastery learning, some secondary teachers worry about the constraint of class time. With limited time available, they fear that the introduction of feedback, corrective, and enrichment procedures will reduce the amount of content they will be able to cover. As a result, they worry that they will have to sacrifice coverage for the sake of mastery.

The first few mastery learning units typically do require more time than usual. Pupils must be provided with some orientation to the process, and class time usually needs to be set aside so the teacher can direct pupils in their corrective work. Teachers who try to have correctives completed as homework or during a special study session before or after school find that those pupils who most need the extra time are the least likely to use it. As a result, it's not unusual for a mastery learning class to be somewhat behind a more traditionally taught class during the first two to three units.

After pupils become familiar with the mastery learning process, however, most teachers find that they can pick up the pace of their instruction.

Mastery learning pupils tend to be engaged in learning activities for a larger portion of the time they spend in class. Hence, they learn more and learn faster in later units than do pupils in more traditionally taught classes (Arlin, 1973; Fitzpatrick, 1985). As pupils catch on to mastery learning, they also tend to do better on their first formative assessments. With fewer pupils involved in correctives and a reduced amount of corrective work required, the class time allocated to correctives in later units can be drastically reduced. Furthermore, because mastery learning pupils learn well the concepts and skills from early units, they are better prepared for later, more advanced units. This means that less time needs to be spent on review activities. Thus, most teachers find that with slight changes in the pacing of their instruction—slightly more time spent in early units but less time in later ones—they are able to cover just as much material as they were able to using more traditional approaches to instruction, and in some cases more (Block, 1983; Guskey, 1983, 1987).

RESEARCH ON MASTERY LEARNING

Implementing mastery learning requires relatively modest changes in teachers' instructional procedures. In most cases, it builds on the practices that teachers have developed and refined over the years. Despite the modest nature of these alterations, however, extensive research evidence shows that the use of mastery learning can have exceptionally positive effects on pupil learning. An extensive, comprehensive review of the research on mastery learning concluded:

> We recently reviewed meta-analyses in nearly 40 different areas of educational research (Kulik & Kulik, 1989). Few educational treatments of any sort were consistently associated with achievement effects as large as those produced by mastery learning. . . . In evaluation after evaluation, mastery programs have produced impressive gains. (Kulik, Kulik, & Bangert-Drowns, 1990, p. 292)

Mastery learning is regularly identified as one of the most effective instructional strategies that teachers can employ at any level of education (Walberg, 1984). Some researchers have even suggested that the superiority of Japanese pupils in international comparisons of achievement in mathematics operations and problem solving may be due largely to the widespread use in Japan of instructional practices similar to mastery learning (Waddington, 1995). Providing feedback, correctives, and enrichments, and ensuring instructional alignment takes relatively little time and effort, especially if the tasks are shared collaboratively among teaching colleagues. Still, results show that the systematic use of these elements helps many more pupils learn well, significantly reduces variation in pupil learning outcomes, and closes gaps in the achievement of different groups of pupils.

Equally important, the positive effects of mastery learning are evident not only in measures of pupil achievement. The process also has been shown to yield improvements in pupils' confidence in learning situations, school attendance rates, involvement in class lessons, attitudes toward learning, and a host of other affective measures (Guskey & Pigott, 1988). This has been referred to as the "multiplier effect" of mastery learning, and makes it an especially powerful tool in school improvement efforts.

CONCLUSIONS

Numerous factors affect pupil learning, many of which lie beyond classroom walls and beyond teachers' control. A recent Educational Testing Service report, for example, identified a wide range of environmental factors that may contribute to achievement gaps, the majority of which are external to schools (Barton, 2003). Denying the role of these outside influences will not endow teachers and schools with the capacity to reduce achievement gaps, and efforts to address these home- and community-based challenges must continue (Rothstein, 2004). Nevertheless, the impediments to learning in pupils' environments *outside* of school should never become a basis for lowering expectations about what can be done to help them learn well *in* school.

The feedback, correctives, and enrichment process, and the instructional alignment elements of mastery learning represent powerful tools that teachers can use to capitalize on the influence they have. Thoughtfully designed formative classroom assessments are a central component in this process. These elements are not, of course, the only factors of importance. In his later writing, Bloom described exciting work on other ideas designed to attain results that were even more positive than those typically achieved with mastery learning, labeling this the "2-sigma challenge" (Bloom, 1984a & 1984b, 1988). Still, careful attention to these elements allows educators at all levels to make great strides in their efforts to reduce variation in pupil achievement and to close achievement gaps. They offer the tools educators need to help *all* pupils learn excellently, including pupils of different racial, ethnic, and socioeconomic backgrounds. As a result, many more pupils learn excellently, succeed in school, and gain the many positive benefits that come from that success.

REFERENCES

Arlin, M. N. (1973). *Rate and rate variance trends under mastery learning.* Unpublished doctoral dissertation, University of Chicago.

Barton, P. E. (2003). *Parsing the achievement gap: Baselines for tracking progress (Policy information report)*. Princeton, NJ: Educational Testing Service.

Block, J. H. (Ed.). (1971). *Mastery learning: Theory and practice*. New York: Holt, Rinehart & Winston.

Block, J. H. (Ed.) (1974). *Schools, society and mastery learning*. New York: Holt, Rinehart & Winston.

Block, J. H. (1983). Learning rates and mastery learning. *Outcomes, 2*(3), 18–23.

Block, J. H., & Anderson, L. W. (1975). *Mastery learning in classroom instruction*. New York: Macmillan.

Bloom, B. S. (1964). *Stability and change in human characteristics*. New York: John Wiley & Sons.

Bloom, B. S. (1968). Learning for mastery. *Evaluation Comment (UCLA-CSIEP), 1*(2), 1–12.

Bloom, B. S. (1973). Individual differences in school achievement: A vanishing point? In L. J. Rubin (Ed.), *Facts and feelings in the classroom*. New York: Walker and Company.

Bloom, B. S. (1974). An introduction to mastery learning theory. In J. H. Block (Ed.), *Schools, society and mastery learning*. New York: Holt, Rinehart & Winston.

Bloom, B. S. (1976). *Human characteristics and school learning*. New York: McGraw-Hill.

Bloom, B. S. (1977). Favorable learning conditions for all. *Teacher, 95*(3), 22–28.

Bloom, B. S. (1984a). The 2-sigma problem: The search for methods of group instruction as effective as one-to-one tutoring. *Educational Researcher, 13*(6), 4–16.

Bloom, B. S. (1984b). The search for methods of group instruction as effective as one-to-one tutoring. *Educational Leadership, 41*(8), 4–17.

Bloom, B. S. (1988). Helping all children learn in elementary school and beyond. *Principal, 67*(4), 12–17.

Bloom, B. S., Hastings, J. T., & Madaus, G. (1971). *Handbook on formative and summative evaluation of pupil learning*. New York: McGraw-Hill.

Fitzpatrick, K. A. (1985, April). *Group-based mastery learning: A Robin Hood approach to instruction?* Paper presented at the annual meeting of the American Educational Research Association, Chicago, IL.

Guskey, T. R. (1983). Clarifying time related issues. *Outcomes, 3*(1), 5–7.

Guskey, T. R. (1987). Rethinking mastery learning reconsidered. *Review of Educational Research, 57*(2), 225–229.

Guskey, T. R. (1997). *Implementing mastery learning* (2nd ed.). Belmont, CA: Wadsworth.

Guskey, T. R. (2000). Twenty questions? Twenty tools for better teaching. *Principal Leadership, 1*(3), 5–7.

Guskey, T. R. (2001). Mastery learning. In N. J. Smelser & P. B. Baltes (Eds.), *International Encyclopedia of Social and Behavioral Sciences* (pp. 9372–9377). Oxford, England: Elsevier Science Ltd.

Guskey, T. R. (2005). Mapping the road to proficiency. *Educational Leadership, 63*(3), 32–38.

Guskey, T. R. (Ed.) (2006). *Benjamin S. Bloom: Portraits of an Educator*. Lanham, MD: Rowman & Littlefield Education.

Guskey, T. R., & Pigott, T. D. (1988). Research on group-based mastery learning programs: A meta-analysis. *Journal of Educational Research*, *81*(4), 197–216.

Johnson, D. W., Johnson, R. T., & Holubec, E. J. (1994). *Cooperative learning in the classroom*. Alexandria, VA: Association for Supervision and Curriculum Development.

Kulik, C. C., Kulik, J. A., & Bangert-Drowns, R. L. (1990). Effectiveness of mastery learning programs: A meta-analysis. *Review of Educational Research*, *60*(2), 265–299.

Kulik, J. A., & Kulik, C. C. (1989). Meta-analysis in education. *International Journal of Educational Research*, *13*(2), 221–340.

Morrison, H. C. (1926). *The practice of teaching in the secondary school*. Chicago: University of Chicago Press.

National Council of Teachers of Mathematics. (2000). *Principles and standards for school mathematics*. Reston, VA: Author. Available online, retrieved May 14, 2006, from: http://standards.nctm.org/document/index.htm.

Rothstein, R. (2004). A wider lens on the black-white achievement gap. *Phi Delta Kappan*, *86*(2), 104–110.

Scriven, M. (1967). The methodology of evaluation. In R. W. Tyler, R. M. Gagne, & M. Scriven (Eds.), *Perspectives of curriculum evaluation* (pp. 39–83). AERA Monograph Series on Curriculum Evaluation. No. 1. Chicago: Rand McNally.

Sternberg, R. J. (1994). Allowing for thinking styles. *Educational Leadership*, *52*(3), 36–40.

Stiggins, R. J. (2002). Assessment crisis: The absence of assessment for learning. *Phi Delta Kappan*, *83*(10), 758–765.

Waddington, T. (1995, April). *Why mastery matters*. Paper presented at the annual meeting of the American Educational Research Association, San Francisco.

Walberg, H. J. (1984). Improving the productivity of America's schools. *Educational Leadership*, *41*(8), 19–27.

Washburne, C. W. (1922). Educational measurements as a key to individualizing instruction and promotions. *Journal of Educational Research*, *5*, 195–206.

Whiting, B., Van Burgh, J. W., & Render, G. F. (1995). *Mastery learning in the classroom*. Paper presented at the annual meeting of the American Educational Research Association, San Francisco.

Wiggins, G. P. (1998). *Educative assessment: Designing assessments to inform and improve student performance*. San Franciso, CA: Jossey-Bass.

CHAPTER 6

Implications of High-Stakes Testing for the Use of Formative Classroom Assessment

Lisa M. Abrams

This chapter examines the implications of federal and state testing policy mandates for teachers' use of formative classroom assessment. It is widely recognized that large-scale state assessments and classroom formative assessments serve different purposes. The goal of large-scale state assessments is to measure the extent to which students have mastered a wide range of curricular objectives and cognitive skills. In contrast, formative assessment is concerned with informing student learning and instructional decision making by using assessments that make the learning process transparent, and in doing so, identify gaps between the current state of learning and the desired learning outcome (Sadler, 1989). Is it possible that the two functions of assessment, the assessment of learning and the assessment for learning, can coexist in a meaningful and coherent way when external accountability pressures are brought to bear on schools, teachers, and students? Before addressing this question, the current context in which teachers deliver instruction, implement assessments, and prepare students for high-stakes tests is explored.

THE EVOLUTION OF HIGH-STAKES TESTING POLICY

It may surprise some readers to learn that the current statewide test-based accountability initiatives grew out of the standards-based reform efforts begun in the early 1990s, not as a direct result of the 2001 No Child Left Behind Act. Standards-based education reform called for a rigorous and demanding curriculum. In addition to requiring students to demonstrate their command of basic content knowledge, this initiative also asked them to exhibit higher-level cognitive processes (e.g., application, problem solving, and inquiry). State legislatures created accountability systems to hold schools, administrators, teachers, and/or students responsible for meeting these raised expectations. These accountability models consisted of four main components (Hamilton, Stecher, & Klein, 2002):

1. Content standards, which communicate the desired content knowledge and skills
2. Tests, designed to measure the progress toward achieving the content standards
3. Performance targets, which identify criteria used to determine whether schools and/or students have reached the desired level of achievement
4. Consequences, such as rewards and/or sanctions based on the attainment of the performance targets

Since the 1990s, test-based accountability systems have become widespread; every state except Iowa has developed content standards (Edwards, 2006a). Moreover, 44 of the states have developed a state-specific test to measure the degree to which students have mastered the knowledge and skills expressed in these standards (Edwards, 2006a). In addition, 13 states use a combination of criterion-referenced and norm-referenced tests designed specifically to measure the state standards, while one state uses a commercially available off-the-shelf test. Although it might appear that state testing policies have become increasingly similar, there are substantial differences in tested content, item format, and the uses of test results especially for the purpose of holding students accountable for performance. For example, 23 states tie graduation to test performance, and eight use student results to make decisions about grade promotion (Edwards, 2006a). As indicated in Table 6.1, the content tested has changed, with more states emphasizing English and math compared to science and social studies over the last several years, although the number of tests that focus on the latter two subjects has grown. The format of state tests has also evolved. Although they were not widespread in the late 1990s, four states used portfolio assessments in 1997. That number decreased to one in 2004–2005. In addition, the Table 6.1 illustrates that the vast majority of states have adopted multiple-choice formats, which are supplemented by short-answer and/or extended-response items in some subject areas and grade levels.

The focus on state assessment requirements was further emphasized in the 2001 reauthorization of the Elementary and Secondary Education Act (ESEA), also known as the No Child Left Behind Act (NCLB). This far-

Table 6.1. Summary of State Test Characteristics 1996–97 to 2004–05: Number of States by Tested Content, Type of Test, and Use of Results for Student Accountability

Characteristics of State Tests		1996–1997	1997–1998	1998–1999	1999–2000†	2000–2001	2001–2002	2002–2003	2003–2004	2004–2005
Tested Content	English	*	35	48	40	44	48	47	48	48
	Math	*	34	47	41	43	48	46	46	47
	Science	*	24	36	25	29	29	34	34	34
	Social Studies	*	17	33	22	23	22	24	22	20
Type and Format of the State Test	Norm-referenced	30	33	29	48	49	48	49	49	49
	Criterion-referenced	31	37	42						
	Writing Assessment/Extended Response in English	33	38	42	34	46	46	44	45	45
	Extended Response in Other Subjects	*	*	*	7	7	18	20	25	28
	Short Answer	*	*	*	37	38	34	32	33	34
	Portfolio Assessment	4	3	2	2	2	2	2	2	1
	Performance Items	15	20	34	*	*	*	*	*	*
Uses of Results for Student Accountability	Graduation and/or Grade Promotion	14	16	21	8	18	17	21	23	24

Source: Edwards, 1997, 1998, 1999, 2000, 2001, 2002, 2003, 2004, 2005.

† In 2000, *Education Week* changed the descriptors of the test format to multiple-choice, short-answer, extended response, extended response in English, and portfolio. The norm-referenced and criterion-referenced categories have been combined to reflect this change. Accordingly, the number of states testing the core content areas indicates the number using criterion-referenced tests to do so. The number of states that used performance items was no longer reported in the yearly Quality Counts special issue.

* Data were not available and/or reported for this category and time period.

reaching legislation sought to raise the level of achievement for all students and to reduce the gap in the performance of students from different backgrounds. At the heart of NCLB are the testing and accountability requirements, which have substantially increased the extent to which students are tested while holding all schools accountable for students' performance. Previous reauthorizations of the ESEA (i.e., the 1994 Improving America's Schools Act) left the states largely responsible for dealing with low- and underperforming schools. In contrast, NCLB requires states to meet Adequate Yearly Progress (AYP) goals to ensure school accountability for student achievement on state tests. If AYP goals are not consistently achieved, schools face increasingly demanding corrective actions (e.g., replacement of school staff, implementation of a new curriculum, extension of the school day or academic year, restructuring) (Joftus & Maddox-Dolan, 2003). It is important to note that the law only prescribes how schools—not students—should be held accountable. Thus, states still retain the authority to determine the level of rewards and/or sanctions at the student-level of accountability.

The implementation of NCLB has expanded a majority of extant state testing programs to more grades and subject areas. Federal law in 2005–2006 required that states administer reading and math tests to all students in grades three to eight and during one year in high school, between the 10th and 12th grades. In addition, a science test requirement was implemented in 2006–2007. The testing mandate affects at least 25 million students annually (Snyder, Tan, & Hoffman, 2004). Arguably, NCLB is one of the most aggressive federal efforts to improve elementary and secondary education by holding schools responsible for student learning and ensuring that all students have an opportunity to learn. The testing requirements that resulted from the earlier statewide accountability provisions and the more recent federal requirements have undoubtedly influenced the content and method of classroom instruction and assessment.

WHAT RESEARCH TELLS US ABOUT THE INFLUENCE OF HIGH-STAKES TESTING ON CLASSROOM PRACTICE

Classroom assessment, particularly formative assessment, is closely linked to the goals and strategies of instruction. To examine how formative classroom assessment can assume a more dominant role in the instructional and learning process, it is necessary to look closely at the context in which formative assessment is used and at how this context is shaped by high-stakes testing programs. It is well documented that high-stakes testing has had mixed and varied effects on the classroom environment, instructional content, and assessment practices, as well as the individuals most closely connected to the instructional process—teachers and students. This next section summarizes much of the research that has been conducted to determine how the implementation of high-stakes testing programs has influenced instruction, learning, and student achievement.

Numerous research studies have investigated the effects of state testing programs, especially those that have high stakes attached to test results. The majority of these studies have involved gathering information from teachers and administrators through the use of surveys, interviews, in-depth case studies, and various combinations of these methods. Typically, research on the influence of state testing programs has focused on single states rather than groups of states. State-level studies have been conducted in Arizona (Smith, Nobel, Heinecke, Seck, Parish, & Cabay, 1997), Colorado (Taylor, Shepard, Kinner, & Rosenthal, 2003), Kentucky (Koretz, Barron, Mitchell, & Keith, 1996a; Stecher, Barron, Kaganoff, & Goodwin, 1998), Maine and Maryland (Firestone, Mayrowetz, & Fairman, 1998), Maryland (Koretz, Mitchell, Barron, & Keith, 1996b; Lane, Park, & Stone, 1999), North Carolina (Jones, Jones, Hardin, Chapman, Yarbough, & Davis, 1999), Texas (Haney, 2000; Hoffman, Assaf, & Paris, 2001), Vermont (Koretz, Stecher, Klein, & McCaffrey, 1994), Virginia (McMillian, Myran, & Workman, 1999), and Washington (Stecher, Barron, Chun, & Ross, 2000), for example. More recently, a national study of teachers has been conducted (Clarke, Shore, Rhoades, Abrams, Miao, & Li, 2003; Pedulla, Abrams, Maduas, Russell, Ramos, & Miao, 2003). The results of the study by Pedulla and colleagues provide the unique opportunity to compare state-level findings with a national perspective on issues related to state-mandated testing programs.

Impact on Classroom Instruction

Teachers make a variety of decisions about what to teach and how to teach. A consistent finding that results from various state-level studies is that teachers have reported giving greater attention to state-tested content areas, sometimes referred to as a "narrowing of instructional content." In examining the impact of Virginia's Standards of Learning (SOL) on the classroom instructional and assessment practices of approximately 700 secondary (English, math, social studies, and science) and elementary school teachers (grades 3–5), McMillan, Myran, and Workman (1999) found that substantial changes in classroom instruction were taking place as a result of the Virginia test. For example, more than 80% of the teachers indicated that the SOL tests had affected the content and pace of instruction rather than the mode or strategies used to deliver information. Further, teachers expressed concern about the breadth of content coverage at the expense of depth of understanding. The pressure to "cover" materials resulted in the elimination of what teachers characterized as "good" lessons and important topics.

A similar study conducted in Maryland examined the impact of the Maryland State Performance Assessment Program (MSPAP) on mathematics instruction (Lane, Park, & Stone, 1999). At the time of the study, the MSPAP had a performance-based assessment component. The MSPAP required students to construct written responses to interdisciplinary tasks that required the application of skills and content knowledge. In order to assess the influence of the MSPAP on the teaching of mathematics, principals, teachers, and students were surveyed at 59 elementary schools and 31 middle schools in grades two to five and seven to eight. A critical component of the research design was to examine teacher responses in tested (3, 5, 8) and non-tested grades (2, 4, 7). In addition to questionnaires, samples of classroom instruction and assessment and test preparation materials were collected and analyzed. The results indicated that MSPAP had a greater influence on mathematics instruction at the lower grades, with elementary teachers placing greater emphasis on learning outcomes.

Research has frequently indicated that increased attention to tested content results in decreased emphasis on other, non-tested, curricular areas (Smith, Edelsky, Draper, Rottenberg, & Cherland, 1991). In Kentucky, 87% of teachers surveyed agreed with the statement that the Kentucky Instructional Results Information Systems (KIRIS) "has caused some teachers to deemphasize or neglect untested subject areas" (Koretz, Barron, Mitchell, & Keith, 1996a, p. 41). Teachers in North Carolina reported similar responses (Jones et al., 1999). Results from a national survey of 4,200 teachers confirm many of these state-level findings. Pedulla and colleagues (2003) reported that 76% of the responding teachers indicated that they had increased the amount of time they spent on tested content areas, while over half of the teachers (52%) reported decreases in the amount of time they devoted to content areas not covered by the state test. Many maintain that this change in focus is appropriate.

In contrast, the impact of the test on instructional strategies is less well understood. Teachers in North Carolina reported mixed effects on instructional strategies. However, studies in states that require students to formulate and provide written responses to test questions show an increased emphasis on teaching writing and higher-level thinking skills (Taylor, Shepard, Kinner, & Rosenthal, 2003). Further, a majority of writing teachers surveyed in Kentucky reported that the KIRIS writing portfolios had a positive impact on writing instruction (Stecher, Barron, Kaganoff, & Goodwin, 1998). Similarly, in a previous study in Kentucky, 80% of teachers reported increasing instructional emphasis on problem solving and writing as a result of the portfolio-based state test (Koretz et al., 1996a).

Although results from survey studies suggest that teachers are tailoring the content of instruction and instructional strategies to mirror the content and format of state tests, other findings suggest a problematic lack of alignment between classroom activities and the cognitive demands of the state test. For example, a content analysis of classroom materials in Maryland (Lane, Park, & Stone, 1999) reported that only half of the materials reflected tasks characteristic of the performance-based MSPAP while the remaining 50% of the instructional tasks consisted of recall and comprehension-oriented computations and word problems. Only a small percentage of the teachers' classroom instructional materials were very similar in terms of the level of problem solving and reasoning skills and the type of explanation and answer format required by the state assessment.

In contrast, results from a national survey of teachers indicated that instructional materials are aligned with the test to a greater degree than did the findings from state-level investigations. Pedulla et al. (2003) reported that a majority of teachers (60%) indicated that the instructional texts and materials that their district requires them to use are compatible with the state test. Further, a larger percentage of teachers (79%) reported that their district's curriculum is aligned with their state-mandated testing program. These large percentages may be the result of increased centralization regarding curriculum decisions and textbook adoption.

Currently, 22 states control the purchase of textbooks rather than allowing such decisions to be made at the local or district level (Manzo, 2003). Both state- and national-level results suggest that a large majority of teachers believe their district and classroom curriculum is aligned to the state test. Research also suggests that this increased alignment requires decreases in attention and time spent on non-tested curriculum (see, for example, Koretz et al., 1996a; Jones et al., 1999; Madaus, 1988; Pedulla et al., 2003; Smith et al., 1991).

Impact on Classroom Assessment

Similar to the findings related to instruction content, research on the influence of state testing programs on teachers' assessment practices indicates that practitioners adapted their own assessments to the format of the state test. In states where tests include open or extended-response items and are focused on higher-level cognitive skills, teachers have reported positive changes to assessment practices and greater emphasis on the quality of their own classroom-level assessments (Borko & Elliot, 1999; Wolf & McIver, 1999). In other states, where most of the test is comprised of multiple-choice or selection-type items, teachers' classroom assessments tend to heavily emphasize these types of questions. Although the item format easily translates from the state test to classroom assessment practices, mirroring the high quality of multiple-choice items designed to measure higher-order thinking skills is challenging to many practitioners. Table 6.2 presents results from a national

Table 6.2. Classroom Assessment Responses of Teachers in High- and Low-Stakes States

Classroom Assessment Practices	In High-Stakes States (%)	In Low-Stakes States (%)
My tests have the same content as the state test.	59	48*
My tests are in the same format as the state test.	51	29*
I use multiple-choice items weekly.	31	17*
I use open-response items weekly.	41	35*
I use extended-response items weekly.	17	9*
I use performance assessments weekly.	12	13
I use group work weekly.	10	9

Source: Pedulla et al., 2003.

* Results are significantly different at $p < .001$

survey of teachers that compared the assessment practices of those in states with high stakes and low stakes attached to results.

As shown, teachers in states with high-stakes tests were significantly more likely to develop and use classroom tests that mirror the content and format of the state test than were teachers in states with minimal consequences for poor test performance. The use of multiple-choice, open, and extended-response items was more frequent in high-stakes contexts—teachers in high-stakes states were twice as likely to report using multiple-choice items on a weekly basis than were their counterparts in low-stakes environments. However, a similarly low percentage of teachers from both types of testing programs reported using performance assessments and collaborative work (approximately 10% respectively).

TEST PREPARATION

The pressure to respond to the increased demands of the state test requires teachers to place more emphasis on preparing students specifically for the state test. In Maryland, 88% of teachers surveyed felt that they were under "undue pressure" to improve student performance on the state test (Koretz et al., 1996b); when asked the same question, 98% of Kentucky teachers responded similarly (Koretz et al., 1996a). Pedulla et al. (2003) found that 90% of teachers reported feeling pressure from their district superintendent to raise test scores, and 79% indicated that they felt pressure from their principal to improve performance on the state test.

Increased emphasis and time devoted to specific test preparation activities is clearly one of the outcomes of the pressure placed on teachers to raise test scores. Of the 470 elementary teachers surveyed in North Carolina, 80% indicated "they spent more than 20% of their total instructional time practicing for the end-of-grade tests" (Jones et al., 1999, p. 201). Similarly, a survey of reading teachers in Texas revealed that, on average, teachers spent eight to ten hours per week preparing students for the Texas Assessment of Academic Skills (TAAS) (Hoffman, Assaf, & Paris, 2001). The most common test preparation activities reported by Texas teachers included demonstrating how to mark the answer sheet correctly, providing test-taking tips, teaching test-taking skills, teaching or reviewing topics that will be on the test, and using commercial test preparation materials and tests from previous years for practice (Hoffman, Assaf, & Paris, 2001, p. 6).

Similar results were found at the national level. Forty-four percent of teachers in high-stakes testing programs indicated that they spent more than 30 hours of instructional time per year preparing students for the state test (Pedulla et al., 2003). As in the Hoffman, Assaf, and Paris (2001) study, Pedulla et al. (2003) found that the most commonly used test preparation activities included teaching test-taking skills, providing students with items similar to those on the state test, and using commercially developed test preparation materials. A moderate emphasis on test preparation, such as familiarizing students with the administration process, format, and structure of the state exam, is considered reasonable. These practices can mitigate heightened levels of anxiety that interfere with student test performance. However, focusing test preparation activities on content measured by the test that have limited applicability to other testing situations is undesirable.

One concern that stems from the reported emphasis on specific test preparation centers on the credibility or accuracy of test scores as a measure of student achievement. Specific test preparation activities, coaching, and instruction geared toward the test can yield scores that are inaccurate (Haladyna, Nolen, & Haas, 1991; Koretz, Linn, Dunbar, & Shepard, 1991; Linn, 1998; Madaus, 1988). For example, one would expect that if students' scores are improving on the state test from year to year, scores on other tests that measure the same content and/or skills will show similar improvement. When trends in student performance levels on similar standardized tests are not consistent, the accuracy of a particular test as an indicator of student achievement is questionable. For example, Pedulla et al. (2003) found that roughly 40% of teachers reported that they have found ways to raise state-mandated test scores without really improving learning.

Similarly, Hoffman, Assaf, and Paris (2001) reported that 50% of Texas teachers surveyed did not think that the rise in TAAS scores "reflected increased learning and high quality teaching" (p. 8). Based on comments provided by the responding teachers, the authors concluded that "teachers regarded improvement on the TAAS as a direct result of teaching to the test" (p. 9).

Consequently, student performance on a highly consequential test may not generalize to other measures of achievement. For example, several studies have compared student performance on other standardized tests that measured similar content knowledge and/or skills. Koretz and Barron (1998) found that the score gains on the KIRIS mathematics test were substantially larger than score gains for Kentucky students on the math section of the National Assessment of Education Progress (NAEP), suggesting that improved performance on the KIRIS math test did not necessarily reflect general gains in student math achievement. Klein, Hamilton, McCaffrey, and Stecher (2000) found similar results when they compared student performance on the TAAS to the performance of Texas students on the NAEP.

Impact on Teachers and Students

Although intended to motivate teachers and students to achieve optimal performance levels, the high-stakes nature of state testing programs can have quite the opposite effect. With regard to teachers, researchers have cautioned that placing a premium on student test performance has led to instruction that is reduced primarily to test preparation, thus limiting the range of educational experiences for students and minimizing the pedagogical skills of teachers (McNeil, 2000; Smith, 1991).

Studies have also concluded that high-stakes assessments increase stress and decrease morale among teachers. According to Jones et al. (1999), more than 77% of the teachers surveyed indicated decreases in their morale. In addition, 76% reported that teaching was more stressful since the implementation of the North Carolina state testing program. Similar results were found in Kentucky and Maryland. Over half of the Maryland teachers and about 75% of Kentucky educators indicated that morale had declined as a result of the state test (Koretz et al., 1996a, 1996b). In addition, 85% of teachers surveyed by Hoffman, Assaf, and Paris (2001) agreed that "some of the best teachers are leaving the field because of the TAAS," thus leading to conclusions that the emphasis on the TAAS was harmful to teaching. Pedulla et al. (2003) reported that one-third of the teachers surveyed nationally indicated that teachers in their school want to transfer out of tested grades.

Although some research identified potentially harmful impacts of high-stakes testing on the morale and professional efficacy of teachers, other studies identified similar concerns for students. Increased levels of anxiety, stress, and fatigue are often seen in high-stakes testing programs, and can have detrimental effects on student performance. According to Pedulla et al. (2003), 73% of teachers surveyed nationally reported that their students were under intense pressure to perform well on their state test. In addition, 76% of those surveyed indicated that students were extremely anxious about taking the test. Of the teachers surveyed in North Carolina, 61% reported that their students were more anxious as a result of the state test (Jones et al., 1999). Similarly, one-third of teachers surveyed in Kentucky indicated that student morale had declined in response to the KIRIS (Koretz et al., 1996a). These circumstances can have a detrimental effect on student engagement, enjoyment of learning, and motivation.

Although some research has found that the high-stakes nature of accountability systems can have a negative influence on morale, climate, and motivation, other studies have yielded dramatically different findings. In these instances, state testing has galvanized teachers to work cooperatively and more effectively to implement higher-quality instruction and assessments (Hamilton, Stecher, & Klein, 2002). For example, teachers involved in the scoring of MSPAP reported that their involvement in the training and scoring process had lead to greater emphasis on reflective practice and a more purposeful approach to their own instruction and assessment practices (Goldberg & Roswell, 1999).

ACCOUNTABILITY AND EDUCATIONAL QUALITY

The majority of research studies on state testing programs have focused on the tests' influence on classroom practices and link changes made by teachers to the pressure to improve test scores. A few studies have directly assessed teachers' views on accountability. In North Carolina, 76% of the teachers surveyed indicated that they "believed that the accountability program would not improve the quality of education in their state" (Jones et al., 1999, p. 202). In contrast, the majority of Kentucky teachers held positive views toward the instructional impact of the state test (Koretz et al., 1996a). However, research conducted in Maine and Maryland suggested that teachers' perceptions of the stakes were not always consistent within a state (Firestone, Mayrowetz, & Fairman, 1998), indicating that consequences attached to test performance can have a differential impact on schools within the same state. In other words, the intended effect of the rewards and/or sanctions tied to test performance may be influenced by other factors specific to schools and districts, such as the availability of resources and professional development opportunities. As a result, state testing policies may produce inconsistent and varied affects across schools and districts (Firestone, Mayrowetz, & Fairman, 1998).

Goertz (2000) specifically addressed accountability issues during a three-year longitudinal study of standards-based reform in eight states. These states included California, Colorado, Florida, Kentucky, Maryland, Michigan, Minnesota, and Texas. During 1998 and 1999, researchers visited 23 school districts to conduct interviews with district staff members who were responsible for accountability and assessment, curriculum and instruction, professional development, low-performing schools, and federal programs. Researchers also visited 57 elementary schools within the 8 states to survey teachers at each school and interview the building principals and the chairs of the school improvement committees. The results of the study led to three main conclusions: 1) Accountability systems provided a clear focus for teachers and principals regarding student learning outcomes; 2) Educators faced few formal consequences for poor student performance; and 3) If formal sanctions were in place, they fell more heavily on students and principals than on classroom teachers (Goertz, 2000). This review of the research on the impact of state-mandated testing programs demonstrates the considerable power these tests leverage on the classroom environment in both positive and negative ways. The changes in climate, instruction, and assessment that results from school, teacher, and student responses to state-mandated testing requirements are complex. Research suggests that the influence of state testing policy is highly variable and does not have the same effect on teachers within the same schools, on schools within the same districts, or on districts within the same state. Based on the review, implications for the use of formative classroom assessment emerge:

1. The content of the state test is a powerful influence on what teachers teach, but not necessarily on how they teach.
2. Classroom assessments mirror the format, item types, and, in some cases, the cognitive demands of the state test.
3. A lack of alignment between instructional materials and the state test suggests a weak, rather than a strong link, between instruction and assessment for classroom purposes and instruction and assessment for the purposes of preparing students for the state test.
4. The focus on increasing test scores rather than learning as the outcome of instruction may promote an overemphasis on specific test preparation strategies, and may detrimentally affect the quality of instruction and assessment, in addition to limiting the efficacy of teachers and the motivation of students in some instances.
5. A reluctance to accept or acknowledge the dominant role of test-based accountability mechanisms may further exacerbate the perceived disconnect between the dual purposes of classroom and large-scale state assessment.

THE ROLE OF FORMATIVE CLASSROOM ASSESSMENT
IN AN ERA OF ACCOUNTABILITY

As described previously, formative classroom assessment strategies ascertain student progress and inform both students and teachers of where students are in relation to the desired learning goal, what changes in knowledge and or skills are needed, and the steps necessary to achieve the goal. In other words, formative assessment makes the learning process transparent. Rather than just measuring what students know and can do, formative assessments, which frequently contain inquiry-oriented or problem-based tasks, uncover the thought process, logic, and understandings students use to arrive at selected answers or narrative responses. The following example illustrates the limitations of large-scale state tests and the utility of formative inquiry.

Interviews with students showed that on the science portion of the Third International Mathematics and Science Study (TIMSS), students had more knowledge about concepts than their written answers had demonstrated for more than half of the test questions. Conversely, the interviews suggested that for one-third of the items, students lacked a sound understanding of the information assessed, even though they had given the correct response (Harlow & Jones, 2003). Greater reliance on formative assessment techniques has the potential to reduce this type of divide between the information produced from a large-scale assessment and that of formative classroom-based assessment, as well as promote stronger linkages between the two (see Chapter 9 of this volume).

Formative assessment strategies can serve multiple purposes and can be especially effective in establishing greater coherence among the varied uses of assessments that inform teachers' decisions about instruction. For example, in today's educational climate, there is heightened attention to and concern about raising classroom and school test scores, but this concern does not necessarily translate to a general emphasis on learning (Elmore & Furhman, 2001). The focus on external accountability test scores can lead to the extensive use of commercially prepared preparation materials, strict emphasis on tested content, and less use of more time-intensive learning activities, such as performance assessments or collaborative projects. Yet research has shown that the use of performance and formative assessment strategies can lead to sizable gains in student achievement, especially for low achievers (Black & Wiliam, 1998; Shepard, 1995, 2000).

In conversations with teachers about their use of formative assessment practices, many have cited that they cannot afford to devote instruction time to these types of activities at the expense of covering the content standards. However, the use of formative, ongoing assessment has been linked to teaching effectiveness. Zemelman, Daniels, and Hyde (1998) concluded that effective teachers have a heightened awareness of the importance of deliberative and systematic approaches to assessment, and place greater value on formative assessment techniques. In addition, McNair, Bhargava, Adams, Edgerton, and Kypros (2003) found that effective teachers did not spend more time on assessment. Instead, they spent a greater proportion of time using formative rather than summative assessment techniques. Further, Stiggins (1999) suggested that use of formative assessment practices can go a long way to increase student motivation and engagement in the learning process. Involving students in monitoring and communicating about their own performance can bring them into the learning process "as partners" by opening up or increasing the transparency of the knowledge and skills required to achieve specific curricular goals.

The use of formative assessment practices by teachers has great potential to not only serve immediate instructional goals but also those of the high-stakes testing mandate. In this context, classroom assessment could serve both formative and summative purposes—a position advocated by Black, Harrison, Lee, Marshall, & Wiliam (2003)—to overcome the implementation barriers to formative assessment use and the perceived inconsistencies among multiple layers of federal, state, and district assessment requirements. Harlen (2005) notes, "there is the potential for such change in the use of computers for assessment, which provide the opportunity for assessment to serve both formative and summative purposes" (p. 213).

Several companies, including CTB McGraw-Hill and Harcourt Assessment, have recognized the potential of connecting formative and summative assessment aims when packaged in the form of computer programs. The development of such computer programs is part of a broader trend among test makers "toward linking large-scale tests with professional development for teachers and more frequent, formative assessments that can be used to support instruction through the year" (Olson, 2006, p. 7). The software systems purport to aid in the diagnosis of strengths and weaknesses in cognitive understandings as well as the prediction of student test performance. For example, in Harcourt's promotional materials, they highlight the capacity of their Learning First program to (1) converge state standards with state-of-the-art technology, (2) raise the bar on formative assessments, (3) bridge the gap between assessment and classroom instruction, (4) discover where students' understanding breaks down, and (5) deliver targeted instruction using high-quality data (Harcourt Assessment Inc., 2005).

Purchasing this type of program is attractive to school districts because it is designed to support the goals of high-stakes testing by providing instructional modules and assessments in a format that appeals to today's computer-savvy students. In addition, the programs provide teachers with specific data that they can use to target instruction. Eduventures, a Boston-based market-research firm, has predicted that this new "formative-assessment market" will generate annual revenues of $323 million for vendors (Olson, 2006).

Although they are described in the same way as the term *formative assessments*, these types of programs are only truly formative in nature if they provide immediate and corrective feedback to students, enabling them to enhance their current level of understanding or skills acquisition and lead to subsequent instruction.

Benchmarking software programs or general database information systems that have typically been used to inform instructional decisions are at best loosely considered formative. Currently, 34 states have interactive school-level databases that can be used by administrators and teachers for analysis and to target instruction (Edwards, 2006b). Although using data in this way informs instructional practice, if it is not accompanied by information that teachers and students can use to correct misunderstandings or extend content knowledge, its use does little to inform students about their own learning.

Formative assessment software, data information systems, or benchmarking programs that do not have the capacity to provide corrective feedback designed to inform the learning process for both teachers and students are more appropriately considered "mini-summative" or "early-warning summative" (Black & Wiliam, 2005) tests rather than formative tools that can be used to support instruction and student learning. Some experts in the field are concerned that *formative assessment* is being redefined as a result of the ubiquitous nature of benchmarking programs that are frequently mislabeled and misunderstood as formative assessments. Chappuis (2005) cautions that the term *formative assessment* is being redefined as a result of the influx and marketing of benchmarking programs and has now come to mean "frequent summative assessments."

The use of data to inform decision making is an effective instructional practice. For example, teachers can use assessment information for making adjustments in their instruction, for grouping students, and for reteaching or remediation activities. However, teachers, administrators, and school division personnel are cautioned against an overreliance on technology that serves summative assessment ends without using formative assessment strategies as a means to achieve these goals.

CONCLUSIONS

This chapter has examined the influence of high-stakes testing programs on the classroom context in which instruction and assessment occur. The research on the effects of tests tied to highly consequential decisions—such as whether an underperforming school is restructured or teachers are transferred to other schools, or if a student will earn a diploma or be promoted to the next grade—is mixed. In some ways, high-stakes testing programs have benefited the educational process, but in other ways, they have yielded unintended negative outcomes. What is clear is that the use of formative assessment can further enhance or extend the positive implications of high-stakes testing programs and mitigate the negative ones, such as decreased levels of student engagement and motivation. At the outset of the chapter, the following question was posed: Is it possible that the two functions of assessment, assessment of learning and assessment for learning, can coexist in a meaningful and coherent way when external accountability pressures are brought to bear on schools, teachers, and students? When classroom instruction and assessment are aligned with the content and cognitive demands of curricular standards as well as with state tests, it is possible to use assessments in ways that support formative and summative purposes. However, achieving this goal requires a shift in the thinking about connections between daily classroom activities and the purpose of high-stakes tests. Rather than acting as two competing purposes, classroom assessment and large-scale assessment can promote the same goal—increased student achievement.

When achievement is viewed as student learning, rather than an increase in test scores, this connection will be more readily apparent. Daily instruction and assessments can serve the purpose of preparing students for the state exam, particularly when both teachers and students are aware of the type of information and skills learners need to be successful in both the classroom and on the state test. This type of information is most effectively provided by the use of formative classroom assessments, from which a wide range of benefits can occur. Greater use of formative assessments will enable teachers and students to work toward achieving the policy aims of test-based accountability while also engaging in thoughtful, effective learning.

REFERENCES

Black, P., Harrison, C., Lee, C., Marshall, B., & Wiliam, D. (2003). *Assessment for learning: Putting it into practice.* Maidenhead, UK: Open University Press.

Black, P., & Wiliam, D. (1998). Inside the black box: Raising standards through classroom assessment. *Phi Delta Kappan, 80*(2), 139–148.

Black, P., & Wiliam, D. (2005). Lessons from around the world: How policies, politics, and cultures constrain and afford assessment practices. *The Curriculum Journal, 16*(2), 249–261.

Borko, H., & Elliot, R. (1999). Hands-off accountability tensions between competing commitments for exemplary math teachers in Kentucky. *Phi Delta Kappan, 80*(5), 394.

Chappuis, S. (2005, August 10). Is formative assessment losing its meaning? *Education Week,* 38.

Clarke, M., Shore, A., Rhoades, K., Abrams, L., Miao, J., & Li, J. (2003). *Perceived effects of state-mandated testing programs on teaching and learning: Findings from interviews with educators in low-, medium-, and high-stakes states.* Chestnut Hill, MA: Boston College, National Board on Educational Testing and Public Policy.

Edwards, V. (Ed.). (1997, Jan. 22). Quality counts: A report card on the condition of public education in the 50 states (*Education Week* special report), 26(17). Bethesda, MD: Editorial Projects in Education.

Edwards, V. (Ed.). (1998, Jan. 8). Quality counts 1998: The urban challenge: Public education in the 50 states (*Education Week* special report), 17(17). Bethesda, MD: Editorial Projects in Education.

Edwards, V. (Ed.). (1999, Jan. 11). Quality counts 1999: Rewarding results, punishing failure (*Education Week* special report), 18(17). Bethesda, MD: Editorial Projects in Education.

Edwards, V. (Ed.). (2000, Jan. 15). Quality counts 2000: Who should teach? (*Education Week* special report), 19(17). Bethesda, MD: Editorial Projects in Education.

Edwards, V. (Ed.). (2001, Jan. 11). Quality counts 2001: A better balance: Standards, tests, and the tools to succeed. (*Education Week* special report), 20(17). Bethesda, MD: Editorial Projects in Education.

Edwards, V. (Ed.). (2002, Jan. 10). Quality counts 2002: Building blocks for success: State efforts in early-childhood education (*Education Week* special report), 21(17). Bethesda, MD: Editorial Projects in Education.

Edwards, V. (Ed.). (2003, Jan. 9). Quality counts 2003: If I can't learn from you . . . Ensuring a highly qualified teacher for every classroom (*Education Week* special report), 22(17). Bethesda, MD: Editorial Projects in Education.

Edwards, V. (Ed.). (2004, Jan. 8). Quality counts 2004: Count me in: Special education in an era of standards (*Education Week* special report), 23(17). Bethesda, MD: Editorial Projects in Education.

Edwards, V. (Ed.). (2005, Jan. 6). Quality counts 2005: No small change: Targeting money toward student performance (*Education Week* special report), 24(17). Bethesda, MD: Editorial Projects in Education.

Edwards, V. (Ed.). (2006a, Jan. 5). Quality counts 2006: A decade of standards-based education (*Education Week* special report), 25(17). Bethesda, MD: Editorial Projects in Education.

Edwards, V. (Ed.). (2006b, May 4). Technology counts 2006: The information edge: Using data to accelerate achievement (*Education Week* special report), 25(35). Bethesda, MD: Editorial Projects in Education.

Elmore, R., & Fuhrman, S. (2001). Holding schools accountable: Is it working? *Phi Delta Kappan, 83*(1), 67–72.

Firestone, W., Mayrowetz, D., & Fairman, J. (1998). Performance-based assessment and instructional change: The effects of testing in Maine and Maryland. *Educational Evaluation and Policy Analysis, 20*(2), 95–113.

Goertz, M. E. (2000, April). *Local accountability: The role of the district and school in monitoring policy, practice, and achievement.* Paper presented at the annual meeting of the American Educational Research Association, New Orleans, LA.

Goldberg, G., & Roswell, B. (1999). From perception to practice: The impact of teachers' scoring experience on performance-based instruction and classroom assessment. *Educational Assessment*, 6(4), 257–290.

Haladyna, T., Nolen, S., & Hass, N. (1991). Raising standardized achievement test scores and the origins of test score pollution. *Educational Researcher*, 20(5), 2–7.

Hamilton, L., Stecher, B., & Klein, S. (Eds.). (2002*). Making sense of test-based accountability in education*. Washington, DC: RAND.

Haney, W. (2000). The myth of the Texas miracle in education. *Education Policy Analysis Archives*, 8(41). Retrieved April 13, 2001 from http://epaa.asu.edu/epaa/v8n41/

Harcourt Assessment Inc. (2005). *Stanford learning first*. San Antonio, TX: Author.

Harlen, W. (2005). Teachers' summative assessment practices and assessment for learning—tensions and synergies. *The Curriculum Journal*, 16(2), 207–221.

Harlow, A., & Jones, A. (2003, July). *Why students answer TIMSS science test items the way they do*. Paper presented at the annual conference of the Australian Science Education Research Association, Melbourne, Victoria, Australia.

Hoffman, J., Assaf, L., & Paris, S. (2001). High-stakes testing in reading: Today in Texas, tomorrow? *The Reading Teacher*, 54(5), 482–494.

Joftus, S., & Maddox-Dolan, B. (2003). *Left out and left behind: NCLB and the American high school*. Washington, DC: Alliance for Excellent Education. Retrieved on May 1, 2003 from http://www.all4ed.org

Jones, M., Jones, B., Hardin B., Chapman, L., Yarbough, T., & Davis, M. (1999). The impact of high-stakes testing on teachers and students in North Carolina. *Phi Delta Kappan*, 81(3), 199–203.

Klein, S., Hamilton, L., McCaffrey, D., & Stecher, B. (2000). *What do test scores in Texas tell us?* (IP-202). Santa Monica, CA: RAND.

Koretz, D., & Barron, S. (1998). *The validity gains on the Kentucky Instructional Results Information System (KIRIS)* (MR-792-PCT/FF). Santa Monica, CA: RAND.

Koretz, D., Barron, S., Mitchell, K., & Keith, S. (1996a). *Perceived effects of the Kentucky Instructional Results Information System (KIRIS)* (MR-792-PCT/FF). Santa Monica, CA: RAND.

Koretz, D., Linn, R., Dunbar, S., & Shepard, L. (1991, April). *Effects of high-stakes testing on achievement: Preliminary findings about generalizations across tests*. Paper presented at the annual meeting of the American Education Research Association and the National Council of Measurement, Chicago, IL.

Koretz, D., Mitchell, K., Barron, S., & Keith, S. (1996b). *Perceived effects of the Maryland school performance assessment program* (Technical Report 409). Los Angeles, CA: CRESST/RAND Institute on Education and Training.

Koretz, D., Stecher, B., Klein, S., & McCaffrey, D. (1994). *The evolution of a portfolio program: The impact and quality of the Vermont program in its second year (1992–93)* (CSE Technical Report 385). Los Angeles: CRESST.

Lane, S., Parke, C., & Stone, C. (1999). *Consequences of the Maryland school performance assessment program*. Washington, DC: United States Department of Education.

Linn, R. (1998). *Assessments and accountability* (CSE Technical Report 490). Boulder, CO: CRESST/University of Colorado at Boulder.

Madaus, G. (1988). The influence of testing on the curriculum. In L. Tanner (Ed.), *Critical issues in curriculum* (pp. 83–121). Chicago: University of Chicago Press.

Manzo, K. (2003, May 21). Lawmakers pursue flexible text selection. *Education Week, 22*(37), pp. 17, 21.

McMillan, J., Myran, S., & Workman, D. (1999, April). *The impact of mandated statewide testing on teachers' classroom assessment and instructional practices.* Paper presented at the annual meeting of the American Educational Research Association, Montreal, Quebec, Canada.

McNair, S., Bhargava, A., Adams, L., Edgerton, S., & Kypros, B. (2003). Teachers speak out on assessment practices. *Early Childhood Education Journal, 31*(1), 23–31.

McNeil, L. (2000). *Contradictions of school reform: Educational costs of standardized testing.* New York: Routledge.

Olson, L. (2006, March 8). ETS buys into formative-assessment market. *Education Week, 25*(26), 7.

Pedulla, J., Abrams, L., Maduas, G., Russell, M., Ramos, M., & Miao, J. (2003). *Perceived effects of state-mandated testing programs on teaching and learning: Findings from a national survey of teachers.* Chestnut Hill, MA: Boston College, National Board on Educational Testing and Public Policy.

Sadler, D.R. (1989). Formative assessment and the design of instructional systems. *Instructional Science, 18*, 145–165.

Shepard, L. (1995). Using assessment to improve learning. *Educational Leadership, 52*(5), 38–43.

Shepard, L. (2000). *The role of classroom assessment in teaching and learning* (CSE Technical Report 517). Los Angeles: CRESST.

Smith, M., Nobel, A., Heinecke, W., Seck, M., Parish, C., Cabay, M. et al. (1997). *Reforming schools by reforming assessment: Consequences of the Arizona student assessment program (ASAP): Equity and teacher capacity building* (CSE Technical Report 425). Los Angeles: CRESST.

Smith, M. L. (1991). Put to the test: The effects of external testing on teachers. *Educational Researcher, 20*(5), 8–11.

Smith, M. L., Edelsky, C., Draper, K., Rottenberg, C., & Cherland, M. (1991). *The role of testing in elementary schools* (CSE Technical Report 321). Los Angeles: CRESST.

Snyder, T., Tan, A., & Hoffman, C. (2004). *Digest of education statistics 2003* (NCES 2005-025). U.S. Department of Education, National Center for Education Statistics. Washington, DC: U.S. Government Printing Office.

Stecher, B., Barron, S., Chun, T., & Ross, K. (2000). *The effects of the Washington state education reform on schools and classrooms* (CSE Technical Report 525). Los Angeles: CRESST.

Stecher, B., Barron, S., Kaganoff, T., & Goodwin, J. (1998). *The effect of standards-based assessment on classroom practices: Results of the 1996–97 RAND survey of Kentucky teachers of mathematics and writing* (Technical Report 482). Los Angeles: CRESST.

Stiggins, R. (1999). Assessment, student confidence, and school success. *Phi Delta Kappan, 81*(3), 191–199.

Taylor, G., Shepard, L., Kinner, F., & Rosenthal, J. (2003). *A survey of teachers' perspectives on high-stakes tests in Colorado: What gets taught, what gets lost.* (CSE Technical Report 588). Los Angeles: CRESST.

Wolf, S., & McIver, M. (1999). When process becomes policy. *Phi Delta Kappan, 80*(5), 401–406.

Zemelman, S., Daniels, H., & Hyde, A. (1998). *Best practice: New standards for teaching and learning in America's schools* (2nd ed.). Portsmouth, NH: Heinemann

Formative Classroom and Large-Scale Assessment: Implications for Future Research and Development

Gregory J. Cizek

Large-scale achievement tests, such as those administered to all pupils in a state under previously existing accountability systems, or those more recently developed in response to the No Child Left Behind Act (NCLB, 2001), are clearly the most visible and deliberated assessment systems today. Classroom assessment, always the bridesmaid, has never received the kind of research or popular attention that its psychometric big sibling has.

Of course, there are some compelling reasons why this would be so. For example, the comparatively greater financial allocation of resources to large-scale testing warrants greater attention to ensure that the investment is well placed. The consequences associated with large-scale testing are often much greater than those associated with classroom assessments. Thus, it seems appropriate that greater attention is paid to ensuring that large-scale tests perform their task of measuring pupil achievement as dependably and accurately as possible. By definition, large-scale assessments are also familiar to a large number of people. In situations, for example, where every pupil in a state must pass a state's high school graduation test, the large-scale test becomes a *lingua franca* for conversations about education for pupils, parents, and policy makers. Finally, the data yielded by large-scale tests facilitate consideration of important public debates about educational progress and reform.

Although large-scale achievement testing focuses nearly exclusively on accountability and coarse-grained summative information about pupil achievement, those interested in formative classroom assessment have diverse perspectives and goals. One set of goals encompasses applied specialists who work for improved classroom assessment as one avenue for enhancing pupil learning (Chappuis & Stiggins, 2002; Stiggins, 2005). Another set of goals is shared by academics who work to establish a more sound scientific foundation for classroom assessment by beginning to suggest what a theory in the area of classroom assessment might look like (Brookhart, 1994, 2003, Chapter 4, this volume; Brookhart & DeVoge, 1999; Rodriguez, forthcoming). An entirely different set of goals is seen in the efforts of those with advocacy or policy interests and who assert that the current situation vis-à-vis large-scale and classroom assessment prominence were precisely the opposite, with assessment attention and resources focused at the level of the educational system closest to the pupil, and the presence and importance of large-scale testing considerably diminished or abolished altogether (see, e.g., Shepard, 2000).[1]

Despite such protestations, it does not appear likely that large-scale testing will decrease in importance, consequence, or prominence. In the balance of this chapter, I describe the current state of relationships between classroom assessment, with its focus on more formative aims, and large-scale achievement testing, and suggest some directions for research that will further clarify this relationship in an effort to improve pupil learning through effective formative assessment. In doing so, I'll build on Chapter 6 to explore additional psychometric issues that impinge upon future studies.

The following sections use common criticisms of large-scale assessments as springboards for examining the linkages to classroom assessment. The criticisms include the charges that large-scale assessments are not helpful for individual pupil decision making, take too much classroom time, are biased, do not take into account pupils' special needs, and are not valid. Using this survey of criticisms, I derive five recommendations for the future of research and practice in the area of formative classroom assessment. Among these recommendations I maintain that formative classroom assessments should:

1. include more explicit linkages to a state's content standards;
2. incorporate systematic assessments for individual pupil diagnosis;
3. become integrated with using a tiered approach to a planned, comprehensive assessment system;
4. incorporate attention to sensitivity and bias reduction; and
5. include attention to appropriate assessment accommodations for pupils with disabilities.

INDIVIDUALLY DIAGNOSTIC ASSESSMENT SYSTEMS

As currently implemented, formative classroom assessments are essentially divorced from large-scale assessments, especially those of the every-pupil variety such as those mandated by NCLB. This is perhaps the area of greatest research need and, hopefully, promise for the future, if only because the current disconnect is so great.

It is becoming increasingly clear that the oft-worried-about effect of large-scale assessments dictating classroom practice is more the exception that the rule (see Abrams, Chapter 6). There is, of course, evidence that large-scale tests drive instruction. For example, if the production of a three-paragraph persuasive essay is required on a state-mandated writing assessment (with even mild stakes attached), it's a good bet that pupils will be taught how to produce such an essay. If a state introduces an elementary-level science test, instruction in science in the elementary grades will likely be intensified (or initiated).

On the other hand, large-scale tests do not appear to be as powerful as drivers of the form or content of local assessments. There is some evidence that teachers (particularly those who participate in item or task development or review for a state assessment) adapt some of those assessment features for classroom assessments (see Cizek, 2001). Nonetheless, although formative classroom assessments *might* be linked more closely to large-scale tests for the purpose of creating a coherent assessment system, they are not as routinely informed or related as might be hoped.

An example from the state of Delaware illustrates this reality. Delaware, which has a total of 18 school districts, provides a comparatively tidy context for examining state assessment policy. On April 8, 2004, Delaware Governor Ruth Ann Minner issued Executive Order Number 54 (EO54), which initiated reviews of various aspects of the Delaware Student Testing Program (DSTP). Among other things, EO54 called for the creation of two review panels. One panel was charged with reviewing the state's content standards, curriculum, and implementation. The second panel was charged with conducting a review of the development of the DSTP assessments, the setting of performance levels, and the design of the pupil accountability system. The most revealing findings were perhaps those of the curriculum panel. In its report, that panel concluded:

> Our panel mostly found what researchers have found in other states that most teachers in Delaware do not have the information and guidance they need to construct and deliver aligned, rigorous lessons and assignments. . . .
>
> We found: There was little consistency among the districts and charters in the guidance they provided to teachers about what to teach. Most districts and charters depend exclusively on a textbook series or program to act as a de facto curriculum framework. Only six districts and one charter school presented curriculum frameworks that were reasonably well aligned with the Delaware standards and that provided the connections among standards, assessments, curriculum and instruction necessary to support effective teaching. (Education Trust, 2005, p. 5)

Alignment of Tests to Standards

In my experience, the findings from Delaware are not unique. As previously noted here and in Chapter 6, some opponents of consequential large-scale assessments might argue that state-mandated tests are overly prescriptive, hegemonic, intrusive, inauthentic, and other bad adjectives. However, even the worst state-mandated tests are reasonably well linked to curriculum/content standards that are usually the result of systematic analysis and negotiation involving educators, policy makers, and the public about what the focus of instruction in a state's classrooms *should* be. The fact that a state's assessments are aligned to these standards is commonly accepted as an essential source of content validity evidence. The fact that classroom instruction is tied to these standards is commonly accepted as another source of validity evidence—a cousin to content validity called "opportunity to learn." Unfortunately, the alignment of formative classroom assessments to the content standards is rare.

The root of this alignment problem can be traced to the lack of exposure to assessment knowledge and skills in most preservice training programs for educators (i.e., teachers, administrators, school counselors, and so forth). What Hills (1991) termed *apathy* toward testing and grading, research on licensure and certification requirements for educators has confirmed—most educators begin their careers with skimpy exposure to the fundamentals of assessment, or worse. At present, most states do not require formal coursework in assessment as a condition of licensure. In addition to the lack of coursework, there often exists a cultural barrier in many university-based education program where large-scale assessment is not viewed favorably and preservice educators are enculturated to oppose such assessments. All things considered, it is not surprising that teachers by and large do not acquire the skills necessary to develop high-quality classroom assessments, much less formative classroom assessments aligned in useful ways to state content standards (see Chapter 2).

Consequently, it does not make sense to talk about assessment *systems* (see Cizek, 1995, and Cizek & Rachor, 1994, for developing planned assessment systems). However, there are some emerging signs that the future holds promise for more coherent integration of what are essentially summative state testing programs used primarily for accountability purposes and the formative assessment activities that happen—or *could* happen—on a daily basis in classrooms. Herein lies the motivation for a first recommendation related to what is arguably the most important frontier for research on formative classroom assessment. Before diving into the recommendation, let us situate the recommendation in the context of a common criticism of large-scale, state-mandated testing; namely, that the results are not terribly useful to classroom teachers.

Subscale Score Differences

At the same time, state-mandated tests have sometimes been promoted by testing companies and policymakers as yielding useful *subscore* results (see Chapter 6), or as diagnostic, when, in fact, because of their length, content coverage, design, and other factors, they are essentially useless when it comes to providing a teacher with specific direction for the next steps to take in providing tailored instruction to any individual pupil (Cizek, 2003). A pupil's performance level (e.g, basic, proficient, advanced) or total score for a content area such as mathematics is, as a rule, highly reliable and accurate. However, the simple fact is that, by design, typical large-scale tests are not designed to yield reliable or accurate information of finer-grain size than the domain covered by the total test. This suggests that teachers and administrators should interpret subscale scores with caution, particularly with individual students.

The limitation can be easily demonstrated by determining the reliability of the differences (r_{DIFF}) obtained between subscale scores. Table 7.1 shows reliability information on a 40-item, state-mandated fourth-grade mathematics test administered each spring to pupils in a large Midwestern state. The state reports pupils' subarea performance using the ubiquitous subscale labels implied by the standards suggested by the National Council of Teachers of Mathematics. For the total test, the estimate of total score reliability is 0.87. That level of reliability permits fairly confident conclusions: If a pupil is classified as proficient vis-à-vis whatever content standards are covered by the mathematics test, then there is a high probability that the pupil is in fact proficient.

Table 7.1. Reliability of Difference Scores, 4th-Grade Midwestern State Mathematics Test

Subtest Name	Number of Items	Reliability
ALGEBRA	4	.40
Data Analysis and Probability	4	.40
Estimation and Mental Computation	3	.33
Geometry	6	.50
MEASUREMENT	8	.57
Number and Number Relations	8	.57
Patterns, Relations, and Functions	3	.33
Problem-Solving Strategies	4	.40

However, teachers have some expectation that a pupil's subscale scores can be used to ascertain, for example, that the pupil is relatively stronger in algebra than measurement, and to focus individual remediation in the weaker area.

Given the few numbers of items in the algebra and measurement subtests (as is typical) and the corresponding skimpy subscale reliabilities, the deck is clearly stacked in favor of an unflattering outcome for the reliability of the differences. The r_{DIFF} for algebra and measurements is .015. However, it might still be surprising that the dependability of conclusions about differences in subarea performance is nearly zero. In many cases, a teacher who flipped a coin to decide whether to provide the pupil with focused intervention in algebra (heads) or measurement (tails) would be making that decision about as accurately as the teacher who relied on an examination of subscore differences for the two areas.

This situation is analogous to the APGAR system in which a value indicating an infant's overall health is assigned shortly after birth. Great confidence can be placed in the overall value, although, if the value is low, it does not convey specific information about the immediate steps that should be taken to improve the infant's health. Rather, the overall value is a signal that more intensive and focused diagnostic assessment must be undertaken. Regarding the total scores on large-scale assessments, although they are highly useful as more general indicators of achievement and are capable of yielding data for informing instruction at classroom, building, or district levels, they are not currently capable of individual diagnosis or prescriptive use—nor are they likely to be.

Some Promising Trends

Some states and testing companies are now beginning to recognize and respond to this shortcoming. Many responses should be tried, but all will need to involve formative classroom assessments. Currently, as pointed out by Lisa Abrams in Chapter 6, some states and publishers of testing and professional development materials are producing formative assessments for local administration and scoring or guidelines for how educators can create performance tasks, scoring rubrics, and other assessment items that are aligned with the state's content standards. Other responses include the development of large item pools (again by states and testing companies) that contain items written to the state's content standards and from which classroom teachers can draw specific subsets of items on demand. The pools need to be large to support inferences about specific skills and to yield accurate information about individual pupils for whom the coarser-grained state test results suggest that additional diagnosis of strengths and weakness is in order.

The most educationally important application of these options is not necessarily as a follow-up to large-scale results. Intact formative assessments and deep, aligned, objective-specific pools for creating teacher-customized formative assessments would be most effectively used as truly formative assessments, as educators apply them to monitor the progress of individual pupils toward mastery of specific content standards in advance of large-scale testing, or as formative information for themselves toward revising general instruction. Some promising work has been begun in the area sometimes referred to as cognitively diagnostic assessment (Nichols, Chipman, & Brennan, 1995). This concept is particularly relevant for the tier of assessments that attempt to help educators better understand a pupil's cognitive organization, to help teachers enhance and tailor instruction, and to provide feedback to pupils about their own learning—all key goals of formative assessment. More research in this promising area would be highly desirable.

In summary, the most striking deficiency of the standards-referenced testing movement is that resource allocation and emphasis on alignment and educationally useful information has been focused almost exclusively on large-scale assessments. That emphasis has yielded high-quality measures for gauging overall achievement, but little information that educators can use to meet the classroom instructional needs of individual pupils. Because, under current circumstances, large-scale assessments *cannot* do this, future research and development should focus on creating additional tiers in a coherent assessment system, each of which would provide information tailored to a specific, different assessment need. An effective, planned assessment and accountability system would integrate the tiers of assessment, all of which would be aligned to the same content standards, as is currently the case with the larger-scale counterparts. However, the system would also incorporate much-smaller-scale assessments that would provide diagnostic information and take into account the format, flexibility, focus, and formative needs of educators.

Finally, the effectiveness of a tiered system that adds a formative assessment component hinges—as does the effectiveness of the current, more limited approach—on the capacity of educators to create, interpret, and use assessment information. It is well documented that many education professionals currently lack preparation in assessment skills. To the extent that new conceptualizations of planned assessment systems take root, educators will need not only the skills to interpret large-scale results, but, perhaps more importantly, skills in creating and using formative assessments to guide individual pupil learning and instructional practices. For any integrated assessment system to function properly, much progress will be necessary to fully and pervasively integrate training in assessment for preservice educators and professional development in assessment for in-service educators.

THE TIME AND COST BURDEN OF ASSESSMENT

The concern that the amount of testing that occurs in American schools has the potential to gobble up limited resources and crowd out valuable instructional time is certainly reasonable. Those who are responsible for large-scale testing programs are acutely aware of this concern and have responded by developing tests that are as efficient as possible in terms of both time and cost. In fact, the very brevity of most tests is a major reason for the subscore (unreliability) problem described in the previous section.

How Much Does Assessment Cost?

Sufficient work has been done to accurately document the extent and cost of large-scale summative testing (see, for example, Goodman & Hambleton, 2005; Phelps, 2000). Although estimates vary fairly wildly, a reasonable approach to the estimation marks the work of the research arm of the U.S. Congress, the General Accounting Office (GAO). The GAO investigated the extent and cost of system-wide (i.e., state- and district-level) testing in 1993. At that time, the GAO estimated that the total number of individual tests administered in elementary and secondary schools each year is 36 million; the per-pupil cost of testing is about $14.50 per pupil ($19.60 in 2005 dollars); and the amount of time devoted to system-wide pupil testing each year was, somewhat surprisingly, only about 3.5 hours per year (United States General Accounting Office, 1993).

The preceding figures and all of the other available research on the topic predate the enactment of NCLB, which has undoubtedly served to increase extent of and expenditures on testing. A more recent GAO report estimating the cost of all testing required under NCLB pegged the total annual expenditure between $271 million and $757 million for the years 2002 through 2008, with the exact amount depending on whether states move toward more cost-efficient selected-response formats or more toward more costly open-ended format items (United States General Accounting Office, 2003).

If the reality in 1993 was that large-scale testing did not devour an inordinate portion of the instructional pie, then the situation has surely changed now that every state is required to test all pupils in grades three through eight and a high school grade annually in reading, mathematics, and science. As NCLB evolves, additional large-scale, every-pupil testing is also a possibility; this would increase the extent to which instructional time is squeezed.

What Constitutes Assessment for Resource Allocation?

On the other hand, it is useful to ask just how big of a squeeze assessment activities really are, and much additional research on this topic is needed.

The answers will depend, in part, on how assessment is operationalized, and on how personal and professional values relate to the proportion of resources that should be devoted to assessment.

The very definition and operationalization of the term *assessment* is somewhat contested territory. Some use the term interchangeably with *test*, although the two clearly have different meanings. A *test* refers to a sample of behavior that is observed and scored under objective, uniform, controlled conditions. Although, to many persons, the definition of *test* calls to mind a specific mode or format (e.g., paper-and-pencil, multiple-choice items, and so forth), such a limited view would be inaccurate. To cite an interesting example, the blood test that a person might obtain during a routine physical examination fits the definition of a *test* that has just been provided. (To be sure, we should all be grateful that such a test requires only a sample and that the conditions are controlled as they are!) A structured observation, an oral questioning, a performance task, a true-false quiz, an interview, or an essay prompt: All of these can be considered *tests*.

An *assessment* differs from a test in that an assessment is the synthesis of various sources of information for the purpose of understanding a pupil's strengths and weaknesses, deciding upon appropriate teaching and learning strategies and experiences, or evaluating progress toward specific educational goals (Cizek, 1997). Preferably, the information to be synthesized is test information, that is, a sample of information collected under controlled conditions so that the dependability, objectivity, utility, meaning, and accuracy of the information are as good as possible.

Viewed broadly, *assessment* is an encompassing term, and the activity pervades life in classrooms. In an early study of teacher decision making, Shavelson and Stern (1981) concluded that teachers make decisions based on assessment information every two to three minutes in the classroom. Stiggins's (1991) work on classroom assessment suggests that teachers spend approximately 35% of their professional lives engaged in assessment-related activities. Thus, although formal, summative assessment activities, such as large-scale state tests, consume only a tiny portion of a pupil's academic year, informal, classroom-tier assessment activity is much more extensive. Whether used for formative or summative purposes, it is clear that the information that is the grist of the assessment mill must be of high quality if important instructional, placement, evaluation, or other decisions are to be made based at least in part on such information.

All told, the extent of information about the time and cost of assessment activities is limited. Defined in differing ways, most of what is known about the extent of assessment pertains exclusively to large-scale, mandated assessments or lumps all assessment-related activities into a single endeavor. It would be helpful to disentangle the relative proportion of time and cost

taken up by summative testing used primarily for accountability and formative assessment activities grounded in classrooms.

Whatever these costs, the amount of spending on assessment remains an
embarrassment. It is likely that in no other field outside education is the financial commitment to understanding the effectiveness of the primary enterprise
so small. For all of the rhetoric about the cost of assessment, the burden is
remarkably light. An analysis by Hoxby (2002) of state spending on assessments used to gather accountability-related information revealed that no state
spent as much as 1% of its elementary and secondary budget on these assessments. In an analysis of all spending on testing in Massachusetts—arguably a
state with one of the most advanced and high-quality pupil testing systems—
Goodman and Hambleton (2005) estimate that only one-third of one percent
of the state's entire education budget was earmarked for testing.

In summary, although funding for assessment activities has—contrary
to rhetoric—been sparse, the lion's share has been channeled into the development and administration of large-scale, summative assessments that primarily target accountability concerns. For the future, although the proportion
of education dollars allocated to all assessment activities should probably
be increased, clearly the greatest need is to develop, broaden, and improve
the quality of formative classroom assessments. At least some portion of this
funding should be targeted directly at educator professional development.

Alternatives to Statewide Testing to Enhance
Formative Assessment

The need for enhanced skill in assessment is motivated by another, related
development that will likely occur. At least among educators, if not the general public, concern exists about increases in large-scale testing (see Phelps,
2005). To the extent that states decide that the assessment of areas other
than those required by NCLB (i.e., reading, mathematics, and science) is
important, the decision about where to locate new assessments in areas such
as writing, history, and other subjects for which state content standards are
developed will be contested. One thing is clear: Not all assessment must be
administered at the state level to yield accountability data, inform instruction, or exert a positive influence on educational practices.

To accomplish some of these aims, a middle tier of assessment should
be considered. For example, states might choose to mandate assessment of
certain curricular areas or content standards developed at the state level (e.g.,
social studies and the arts) and might even provide rules, guidelines, or recommendations regarding the scope, content, format, and achievement-level
descriptions for those assessments, while leaving test development, schedul-
ing, administration, and reporting of results as a local responsibility. If desired, monitoring of the local assessments could be instituted, or states might

require the submission of assessment frameworks, sample assessments, scoring guides, performance standards, and results reported using achievement levels for aggregation and reporting at the state level.

The latter strategy may be particularly effective in assessing currently unassessed content areas, or portions of currently assessed areas for which certain content standards are not easily measured in large-scale contexts. Few states have actually demonstrated that such a system can work, although some (notably New Jersey and Ohio) are experimenting with a tiered approach in which state and local assessment activities are coordinated. The approaches are promising, and research will be needed to determine the most effective and efficient ways to align the formative and summative components.

TEST BIAS

Another research opportunity for those in the area of classroom assessment is found at the as-yet underexplored intersection of classroom assessment and strategies for identifying, avoiding, and addressing differential item functioning (DIF) and potential item and test bias.[2]

To date, it is accurate to say that the sole focus of psychometricians concerned about unfairness in assessment has been on large-scale testing. For example, the chapter on Bias in Test Use (Cole & Moss, 1989) in the authoritative reference in the field of educational measurement, *Educational Measurement*, 3rd ed., focuses exclusively on large-scale testing contexts. Almost only statistical, the applications of bias detection methods (e.g., factor analytic approaches, chi-square approaches, comparisons of item characteristic curves, and so on) that are described in this resource can be applied only in situations of the largest scale. A reader of that chapter—or, essentially, any of the DIF/bias literature since the publication of that chapter—could reasonably conclude that: 1) classroom assessment does not occur; or 2) classroom assessments occur, but they are not affected by the threat of construct-irrelevant variance (a new edition of *Educational Measurement* is being prepared).

Even textbooks in educational measurement that are geared primarily toward preservice and in-service teachers—that is, those who develop and use classroom assessments—are noticeably devoid of information on classroom assessment bias. One recent textbook for teachers states:

> Classroom teachers need to know that assessment bias exists. Assessment bias in [large-scale] educational tests is probably less prevalent than it was a decade or two ago. . . . However, for the kinds of teacher-developed assessment procedures seen in typical classrooms, systematic attention to bias eradication is much less common. (Popham, 2002, p. 86)

Despite this observation, the few pages on assessment bias are primarily devoted to the context of large-scale assessment, including consideration of disparate/adverse impact, bias review panels, and empirical DIF detection. The complementary practical direction for teachers to follow in their own test construction and evaluation activities is far less well developed.

Most measurement specialists would probably concur with Popham (2002) on the stark contrast between large-scale and classroom assessments when it comes to their technical quality. It is probably not an exaggeration to say that a large-scale, state-mandated mathematics test required for high school graduation carries the strongest evidence of content validity, is the most carefully scrutinized, bias-free, dependable, efficient, and fair test that a pupil will take in his or her educational career. On the other hand, the teacher-created performance assessment, individual pupil interview, observation of group work, assigned term paper, or formative quiz is comparatively and considerably more subjective, multidimensional, bias-laden, and unreliable (it is technically more correct to say that the scores, not the tests, are unreliable).

On a more positive note, I suspect that one of the unintended consequences of all the attention being paid to fairness in large-scale (e.g., state-level) pupil achievement testing is that a trickle-down effect will bring knowledge about high-quality measurement and concerns about fairness into the classroom assessment realm (see Cizek, 2001). One example of this is found in the current work on the effects of reducing the linguistic complexity in assessments, particularly mathematics assessments, by Abedi and his colleagues (see, e.g., Abedi, Courtney, & Leon, 2003; Abedi, Hofstetter, & Lord, 2004). Preliminary findings indicate that modifications to non-content-area-related vocabulary, sentence structure, and so on do not affect the integrity of the construct being assessed.

Debunking the notion that educators' classroom assessment practices—particularly those that are least formal and would be considered most formative in nature—are inherently untainted by observer and scoring (broadly defined) bias will be a hurdle to overcome. A first step in this research agenda will be to conduct the observational and descriptive studies necessary to identify the extent and nature of the problem. A second necessary step will be the development of field-based techniques that educators can use to detect and reduce the extent of bias in formative classroom assessments. Because of the substantial differences in context, purpose, format, and other characteristics that distinguish large-scale summative and formative classroom assessments, the techniques developed for classroom use will almost surely be less quantitative and rooted in probability theory. A third necessary step will likely be to determine the extent to which the techniques improve classroom assessment; namely, the degree to which attention to bias in classroom assessment is disseminated and incorporated into both preservice training and professional development experiences.

ASSESSMENT ACCOMMODATIONS

The positive validity benefit of reducing linguistic complexity was mentioned in the previous section. Such attempts to reduce construct-irrelevant test score variance (i.e., bias) can also be thought of as a testing accommodation. More generally, however, it may be useful to think of bias reduction measures as those steps that are taken during the test development or scoring process, whereas test accommodations can be thought of as those steps related to the test production and administration phases; for example, large-print forms, additional testing time, frequent breaks, the use of readers or scribes, and so forth. Thurlow and Thompson (2004) have provided a concise classification system for thinking about assessment accommodations. Table 7.2 shows a listing of assessment accommodations and examples of each type drawn from Thurlow and Thompson's work.

Just as concerns about fairness must trickle down to classroom assessments to a greater degree than previously, concerns about appropriate accommodations —made salient with the arrival, increase, and importance of higher-stakes tests— are relevant for classroom assessment. In some states, the only accommodations permitted are those that the pupil routinely receives as a part of regular classroom assessment. For example, according to a test administration manual related to the Texas Assessment of Knowledge and Skills (TAKS) tests:

Table 7.2. Categories and Examples of Test Accommodations

Accommodation Type	Example
Setting Accommodation	Provide accessible furniture, individual or small-group administration
Timing Accommodation	Allow extra time, frequent breaks during testing
Scheduling Accommodation	Administer test over several sessions, different days or times
Presentation Accommodation	Provide test in audiotape or large-print version
Response Accommodation	Allow scribe to record pupils' answers, permit oral responses
Other Accommodation	Permit use of highlighters, reading rulers, or other aids

Source: Adapted from Thurlow and Thompson, 2004.

The decision to use a particular accommodation with any pupil should be made on an individual basis and should take into consideration (a) the needs of the pupil and (b) *whether the pupil routinely receives the accommodation in instruction and testing.* (Texas Education Agency, 2004, p. 61, emphasis added)

Clearly, educator familiarity with the accommodation options and appropriateness of each as an important aspect of regular instructional planning is vital, as is sensitivity to accommodations (modifications) that threaten the inference or interpretations that a specific test is designed to yield. This applies to classroom assessments as well as to larger-scale testing. For the results of classroom assessments to yield the kinds of interpretations that a teacher desires to make, appropriate accommodations must be in place for pupils who require them. Inappropriate accommodations should not be provided in cases where they alter the meaning of the assessment information.

Despite some excellent work identifying the psychometric, legal, and policy issues involved (see, e.g., Pitoniak & Royer, 2001; Sireci, Scarpati, & Li, 2005), the state of research on what constitutes an appropriate accommodation for a given pupil on a large-scale assessment is still in its comparative infancy—which would mean, by extension, that the state of affairs in classroom assessment accommodations is essentially embryonic. Whereas there are often sound, specific, published guidelines provided to educators regarding what constitutes an appropriate accommodation for a large-scale test, no such guidelines are routinely provided to help educators understand the nature and effect of accommodations for formative assessments that are used for daily classroom information-gathering. For the future, research on appropriate classroom accommodations is necessary. As has been noted in previous sections, the efficacy of dissemination and professional development will be key to helping educators incorporate accommodations that yield accurate assessment information.

CONCLUSIONS

The recent, increasing prominence of large-scale pupil achievement testing has overshadowed the role and importance of classroom assessments. And, at least in the near term, it does not seem likely that large-scale testing will decrease in frequency, importance, or consequence. However, in contrast to the comparatively advanced state of research and practice vis-à-vis the technologies of large-scale testing, formative classroom assessment remains an area of much promise, underdeveloped linkages to large-scale assessment, and vital contribution to fostering pupil achievement. Common criticisms of large-scale assessments must be addressed, but addressing them in ways that promote greater understanding of large-scale testing offers the benefit of promoting stronger relationships, research, and practice in classroom assessment as well.

To enhance the utility, educational importance, and power of formative classroom assessments, they must be linked to accepted content standards; integrated into a coherent, comprehensive assessment system; yield individually diagnostic information that teachers can use; avoid bias; and incorporate appropriate assessment accommodations. Clearly, this is a tall order—especially in the context of current professional training that is persistently weak in terms of providing key assessment training for educators. However, just as the recognition of the role and importance of high-stakes tests has resulted in many educators becoming more familiar with measurement principles in that context, recognition of the power and utility of sound formative assessment at the classroom level may also help spur increased attention to this assessment frontier.

NOTES

1. I have described this extreme position in another place, referring to the *jihad* rhetoric of the abolitionists (see Cizek, 1990, 2003), who reject consequential decision making associated with test performance. The work of Shepard (2000) cited here provides an illustrative case. In an ostensibly complete theoretical explication of the role of assessment, curriculum, and learning theory, no assessment beyond the classroom level is included. In fact, even the classroom assessment in Shepard's model does not permit any consequences: The only classroom assessments included are used formatively. (See Figure 4 in Shepard, 2000, p. 8.) The associated rhetoric is representative of this advocacy/policy genre:

> If we wish to purse seriously the use of assessment *for* learning . . . it is important to recognize the pervasive negative effects of accountability tests and the extent to which externally imposed testing programs prevent and drive out thoughtful classroom practices. In presenting these ideas to an audience of educational researchers and teacher educators, I used the image of Darth Vader and the Death Star to convey the overshadowing effects of accountability testing. (p. 9)

2. This section on bias, and the following sections on accommodations and validity, could all have been subsumed under the most encompassing term of the three: *validity*. However, for the sake of distinguishing among three differing emphasis areas for future research and practice in classroom assessment, they are treated here as more distinct than they truly are.

REFERENCES

Abedi, J., Courtney, M., & Leon, S. (2003). *Research-supported accommodations for English language learners in NAEP* [CSE Technical Report No. 586]. Los Angeles: UCLA Center for the Study of Education.

Abedi, J., Hofstetter, C. H., & Lord, C. (2004). Assessment accommodations for English language learners: Implications for policy-based empirical research. *Review of Educational Research, 74,* 1–28.

Brookhart, S. M. (1994). Teachers' grading: Practice and theory. *Applied Measurement in Education, 7*(4), 279–301.

Brookhart, S. M. (2003). Developing measurement theory for classroom assessment purposes and uses. *Educational Measurement: Issues and Practice, 22*(4), 5–12.

Brookhart, S. M., & DeVoge, J. G. (1999). Testing a theory about the role of classroom assessment in pupil motivation and achievement. *Applied Measurement in Education, 12*(4), 409–425.

Chappuis, S., & Stiggins, R. J. (2002). Classroom assessment for learning. *Educational Leadership, 60*(1), 40–43.

Cizek, G. J. (1990, April 4). The sloppy logic of test abolitionists. *Education Week, 64.*

Cizek, G. J. (1995). The big picture in assessment and who ought to have it. *Phi Delta Kappan, 77*(3), 246–249.

Cizek, G. J. (1997). Learning, achievement, and assessment: Constructs at a crossroads. In G. D. Phye (Ed.), *Handbook of classroom assessment* (pp. 1–32). San Diego, CA: Academic.

Cizek, G. J. (2001). More unintended consequences of high-stakes testing. *Educational Measurement: Issues and Practice, 20*(4), 19–27.

Cizek, G. J. (2003). Rejoinder: E. *Educational Measurement: Issues and Practice, 22*(1), 40–44.

Cizek, G. J., & Rachor, R. E. (1994). The real testing bias: The role of values in educational assessment. *NASSP Bulletin, 78*(560), 83–93.

Cole, N. S., & Moss, P. A. (1989). Bias in test use. In R. L. Linn (Ed.), *Educational measurement* (3rd ed.) (pp. 201–220). Washington, DC: Macmillan.

Education Trust. (2005, February). *Delaware math curriculum frameworks review.* [Report in response to Executive Order 54.] Washington, DC: Author.

Goodman, D., & Hambleton, R. K. (2005). Some misconceptions about large-scale educational testing. In R. P. Phelps (Ed.), *Defending standardized testing* (pp. 91–110). Mahwah, NJ: Erlbaum.

Hills, J. R. (1991). Apathy concerning grading and testing. *Phi Delta Kappan, 72,* 540–545.

Hoxby, C. M. (2002). The cost of accountability. In W. M. Evers & H. J. Walberg (Eds.), *School accountability* (pp. 47–73). Stanford, CA: Hoover Institution.

Nichols, P. D., Chipman, S. F., & Brennan, R. L. (Eds.). (1995). *Cognitively diagnostic assessment.* Mahwah, NJ: Erlbaum.

No Child Left Behind Act. (2001). P. L. 107-110, 20 U.S.C. 6301.

Phelps, R. P. (2000). Estimating the cost of standardized pupil testing in the United States. *Journal of Education Finance, 25,* 343–380.

Phelps, R. P. (2005). Persistently positive: Forty years of public opinion on standardized testing. In R. P. Phelps (Ed.), *Defending standardized testing* (pp. 1–22). Mahwah, NJ: Erlbaum.

Pitoniak, M. J., & Royer, J. M. (2001). Testing accommodations for examinees with disabilities: A review of psychometric, legal, and social policy issues. *Review of Educational Research, 71*(1), 53–104.

Popham, W. J. (2002). *Classroom assessment: What teachers need to know*. Boston: Allyn and Bacon.

Rodriguez, M. (forthcoming). *Toward a theory of classroom assessment*. Manuscript in preparation. University of Minnesota, Department of Educational Psychology.

Shavelson, R. J., & Stern, P. (1981). Research on teachers' pedagogical thoughts, judgments, decisions, and behavior. *Review of Educational Research, 51*(4), 455–498.

Shepard, L. A. (2000). The role of assessment in a learning culture. *Educational Researcher, 29*(7), 4–14.

Sireci, S. G., Scarpati, S. E., & Li, H. (2005). Test accommodations for pupils with disabilities: An analysis of the interaction hypothesis. *Review of Educational Research, 75*(4), 457–490.

Stiggins, R. J. (1991). Relevant classroom assessment training for teachers. *Educational Measurement: Issues and Practice, 10*(1), 7–12.

Stiggins, R. J. (2005). *Pupil-involved assessment for learning*. New York: Prentice Hall.

Texas Education Agency. (2004). *ARD committee decision-making process for the Texas assessment program: Reference manual for the 2004–2005 testing year*. Austin, TX: Author.

Thurlow, M. L., & Thompson, S. J. (2004). Inclusion of pupils with disabilities in state and district assessments. In G. Walz (Ed.), *Measuring up: Assessment issues for teachers, counselors, and administrators* (pp. 161–176). Austin, TX: Pro-Ed.

United States General Accounting Office. (1993). *Pupil testing: Current extent and expenditures with cost estimates for a national examination* (Report No. PEMD-93-8). Washington, DC: Author.

United States General Accounting Office. (2003). *Characteristics of tests that will influence expenses: Information sharing may help states realize efficiencies* (Report No. GAO-03-389). Washington, DC: Author.

CHAPTER 8

Formative Classroom Assessment in Science and Mathematics

Wynne Harlen

This chapter considers the practical steps involved in implementing formative assessment in learning and teaching science and mathematics. It opens with a brief rationale for the important role that formative assessment plays in the learning and teaching of science and mathematics. This involves some discussion of the nature of understanding in these subjects and how it differs from surface knowledge of facts and algorithms. The process of learning is seen as the progressive development of understanding, in which new experience is linked to existing frameworks. The role of process or inquiry skills in this learning is emphasized, leading to the recognition that, to support learning, teachers need to gather information about relevant existing skills and ideas, interpret this in relation to what it means for the pupils' next steps in learning, and then find ways to help pupils take these steps. It is also argued that pupils have a central role in these processes. The later sections look, in turn, at how teachers can put these processes into action in the science and mathematics classroom. The chapter concludes with some points about managing formative assessment and acknowledges some challenges to implementation.

THE GOALS OF LEARNING IN SCIENCE AND MATHEMATICS

In science and mathematics education, as in most other areas of education, there is now a widespread recognition that subjects consist of more than just their "facts." What is involved with the process of thinking about a subject and deep understanding is as much part of what the pupil is learning as is the more traditional content knowledge. Although learning processes in detail vary among subjects, underpinning learning in all subjects is a view of learning as the progressive development of understanding, in which new experience is linked to existing knowledge. Harlen and James (1997) put it this way:

> The identification and creation of links to existing frameworks depend on the active participation of the pupil and on the familiarity of the context of the material to be learned. Understanding, in this view, is the process of construction and reconstruction of knowledge by the pupil. (p. 368)

These processes take place in a social context (Driver & Scott, 1995) where interaction between the pupil, the teacher, and others within and beyond the classroom has a key role in the development of ideas.

This view of learning places the pupil at the center of the process and, at the same time, provides a rationale for the formative use of classroom assessment. To foster learning in this way, teachers need to know what the pupils' existing frameworks are so that they can adapt further learning experiences to be within the capacity of pupils to form links to these frameworks. Equally important, pupils should know where they are in relation to the goals of learning. Pupils do the learning, and they need to be able to direct their effort appropriately. This, in turn, means that pupils should understand the goals of their work.

In science, the goals of learning are a combination of the development of conceptual understanding, skills of investigative inquiry, and scientific attitudes. For students, the linking involves using their own and others' ideas to try to make sense of new experience, a process that involves making a prediction and considering whether the evidence of the new experience supports the prediction. This means gathering, interpreting, and communicating relevant data; in short, using the skills of inquiry. In this process, ideas are extended to encompass more experience, and the ideas become more widely applicable, more useful, and more abstract. The relevant point in the present context is that the development of understanding depends on the use of inquiry skills (and the attitudes that energize their use), and so these skills have to be developed and used scientifically. Consequently, classroom assessment that helps learning in science must encompass concepts, skills, and attitudes.

The process of doing mathematics can be divided into strands such as problem solving, communicating, and reasoning. The problem-solving strand involves the development of skills for making decisions about how to use mathematical knowledge when tackling a problem. It involves progressively greater independence in the approach to mathematical problem situations.

The communication strand tackles the issues of pupils communicating the mathematics they are doing and also of understanding the mathematics presented to them.

The reasoning strand involves justifying, generalizing and, ultimately, proving mathematical results. The parallels can easily be seen between these skills and those identified in science.

These skills are by no means limited to the curriculum areas of science and mathematics. They are part of the general thinking skills embedded in a modern curriculum, usually taken to include information-processing, reasoning, creative thinking, evaluation, and inquiry skills. These key skills support continued learning, recognized as essential in the world of rapid change for which today's pupils must be prepared. Given these priorities for pupils' learning, the assessment processes used in classrooms need to be ones that support and promote these skills as well as the development of concepts and attitudes. What this means in practice is that the teacher has to:

- find out how far pupils have reached in relation to the goals of the work,
- decide what the next appropriate steps are in learning,
- help pupils to take these next steps, and
- involve pupils in these decisions.

The rest of this chapter considers ways in which this can happen in the context of science and mathematics. Although they are discussed separately, in practice, the processes of gathering, interpreting, and using evidence are often very similar. Although the involvement of pupils in formative assessment is discussed later, it is emphasized that pupil involvement has a central part in developing pupils' autonomy (see Chapter 9, this volume).

WAYS OF GATHERING EVIDENCE OF PUPILS' IDEAS AND SKILLS

Teachers use several methods, often in combination, to gather evidence about their pupils' achievement in relation to the learning goals. The main ones are questioning, discussion, dialogue and listening to students' talk; studying the products of tasks, including tests, that are designed to reveal pupils' thinking; and observing pupils' actions. Questioning, discussion, and dialogue also have important roles in helping pupils take their next steps, as will be discussed later.

Questioning

Questioning is a major part of teachers' classroom interactions with pupils, and it plays a key role in classroom assessment. However, as Black, Harrison, Lee, Marshall, and Wiliam (2002) point out, many teachers do not plan what to say and what questions to ask. Two main aspects of questioning practice are considered here to encourage teachers to plan their question-asking more explicitly. One is the framing of the question asked; the other is about timing, particularly the time allowed for answering.

When the purpose of questioning is to find out pupils' ideas and how pupils are linking new experience to their existing mental frameworks, the questions should invite more than a one-word answer; they should encourage pupils to say what they really think, not to guess what answer the teacher is looking for. Changing a question from, for example, "Why do we need food?" to "Why *do you think* we need food?" makes a significant difference in the kind of answer pupils feel is required. The latter question gives an invitation to pupils to express their own ideas, while the former suggests that a particular answer is expected. The same change can be made when the response is not a spoken answer to a question but a piece of written work or a drawing. For instance, if the teacher instructs pupils, "Draw what you think is happening inside the incubating egg," the result is more likely to help the teacher to identify the ideas pupils have than asking for a drawing of the egg would be.

Similarly, in mathematics, the answer to a question such as "Is 7 a prime number?" will give the teacher less information about a pupil's thinking than a question like "Why do you think 7 is an example of a prime number?" (Qualifications and Curriculum Authority [QCA], 2001, p. 11). The latter requires pupils to explain and justify their reasoning and does not require follow-up questions in order to obtain a wider range of evidence.

Questions of the following types require pupils to think, not about whether they can recall a "fact," but about what they know about a situation and its general properties. Such questions will provide far more formative information and also perhaps enable pupils to extend or deepen their understanding—genuine assessment FOR learning. Here are some examples based on Watson and Mason (1998):

Is it always true that . . . ?
Is it ever false that . . . ?
How many different ways can you find to . . . ?
Give me a definition of . . . in your own words.
What is the same and what is different about . . . ?
What is wrong with the statement . . . ?
What other information do you need to solve this problem . . . ?

The timing of questions, and particularly the time allowed for answering, is equally important. Research shows that teachers typically allow one second for answers to a question before either rephrasing the question or answering it themselves (Rowe, 1974). This is short even for questions that require only recall, and well-thought-out questions, which require pupils to give explanations or express their ideas, take much longer to answer. One of the significant changes in practice that Black et al. (2002) reported from their work with teachers was to increase "wait" time after asking a question. Some teachers gave time for pupils to talk in groups before asking for responses to a question; others told pupils not to raise their hands, since all pupils were expected to be able to give an answer of some kind; others made a point of discussing and using "wrong" answers to show that these were as useful in learning as correct ones. In all cases, the teachers received answers that enabled them to develop the pupils' ideas more effectively and also to involve all pupils as active participants in learning. These teachers were actively seeking evidence from and about the pupils that would enable them to adjust their teaching, which is the essence of formative assessment.

Discussion and Dialogue

Pupils' talk is a very valuable source of evidence about their thinking. It is also an important means of helping the development of deep understanding, as will be discussed further in relation to helping pupils take the next steps in their learning. The words that pupils use in talking with one another often give evidence of their ideas. Therefore, it is particularly useful to set up a situation in which pupils converse with each other while the teacher "listens in" without participating in the discussion. One way of doing this is to use "concept cartoons." These are cartoon drawings that show an object or event being discussed by three or four pupils. Each has a "speech bubble" in which different views about how to explain the event are suggested. These views reflect common misconceptions as well as the correct explanation. The originators of the concept, Keogh and Naylor (2000), have produced a number of such cartoons on different science topics. Either in groups or as a class, the pupils discuss the ideas suggested by the cartoon characters, talk about why they agree or disagree with the suggestions, and give their own ideas. Another approach is to group the pupils and assign work on a combined concept map (Novak & Gowan, 1984) where they have to agree on how to connect a selection of concept words relating to the topic being studied.

By listening to students' talk, the teacher may find that pupils are using words in a context that suggests that their meaning is not understood. For instance, in science, melting and dissolving and reflection and shadows are often confused. In such cases, the teacher can explore the meaning pupils give to these words, perhaps by asking them to give an example of something "melting."

Studying Pupil Work Products

Pupils' writing, drawings, and other artifacts can be a rich source of evidence about their ideas and skills, providing that 1) the task is set up so that they have to express their ideas, and 2) the teacher notices the significant features of the work. The task needs to be set up so that pupils have to express what they think is happening or how they would explain something, rather than just to draw or write about what they see. The points made earlier about asking questions also apply here.

Studying pupils' products carefully with a diagnostic eye takes time. If work is only considered superficially, it is easy for the teacher to overlook evidence that could help decide how to help further learning. A few well-designed tasks that are carefully reviewed by teachers are worth more than a greater number that either do not require much thinking or from which the teachers learns little about students' thinking.

Advice to primary (elementary) school mainstream teachers (Association for Science Education (ASE), 2002) makes similar points and also urges teachers to be clear about the evidence of pupils' thinking before responding; in other words, to read work carefully and try to understand what the pupil is saying before responding. For example, if a student writes, "When you pluck the string or bang the drum it makes the sound, but when you blow the bottle you are making the sound," the teacher might ask the student to say more about what he was doing when he blew across the bottle and whether he thought there would be a sound without the bottle. With that clarified, the student might be asked to think about what happens when the string is plucked or the drum hit to help him recognize that blowing also made something move.

With some topics, the teacher can gain a quick overview of the ideas of all pupils by collecting their reports together, as in this example:

> One teacher, in planning a lesson on simple circuits, decided to have the pupils draw on the whiteboard all the circuits they tried to construct, both those that did and those that didn't work. This form of communication gave her an immediate picture of the way the pupils' ideas were developing and enabled her to work with those who were unsure and needed help in understanding what is essential in a complete circuit. (Institute for Inquiry, 2003, p. 22)

Observing Pupils' Actions

Although pupils' written work can be used to provide evidence of their skills, it rarely provides the detail that is necessary to judge whether or how certain skills have been used. Observation of how pupils are working provides useful insight into their inquiry skills and attitudes. For example, in science, how pupils make changes in their investigation of variables and in mathematics how they read scales, draw graphs, and use number grids will provide needed detail. In fact, almost everything pupils do gives some evidence of their thinking. Therefore, it is necessary to be able to identify the behavior that is of most significance. It helps a teacher to have in mind some indicators of what to look or listen for in relation to the goals of learning. Moreover, if these indicators describe progress toward the goals, then they also help in identifying the next steps in learning.

DECIDING NEXT STEPS

Although not enough is definitively known about the course of development of some learning outcomes, research into pupils' learning in science and mathematics and classroom experience enables frameworks of progression to be mapped out in mathematics and science, perhaps more feasibly than in social subjects (see Chapter 9, this volume). The results have been variously described as "progress maps" (Masters & Forster, 1996), "developmental indicators" (Harlen, 2006), and "progress variables" (Wilson, Kennedy, & Draney, 2004). As an example, the indicators for "interpreting evidence and drawing conclusions" are expressed in terms of statements of what pupils are able to do, with the developmental progression from statement 1 to 7 (Harlen, 2006):

1. Compare what they find with what they predicted or expected.
2. Identify patterns or trends in their observations or measurements.
3. Draw conclusions that summarize and are consistent with all the evidence that has been collected.
4. Discuss what they find in relation to their initial question or hypothesis.
5. Use patterns to draw conclusions and attempt to explain them in terms of scientific concepts.
6. Recognize that there may be more than one explanation that fits the evidence.
7. Recognize that any conclusions are tentative and may have to be changed in the light of new evidence.

(p. 107)

The statements in the *Content Standards for Science Education* (National Research Council [NRC], 1995) can be regarded as rather coarse-grained progress maps, as can the levels of attainment in the National Curriculum for England (Department for Education and Skills [DfES], 1999) and similar documents. However, for the purpose of using classroom assessment to help learning, there is no need to relate to stages or levels. What is important is to describe how a skill or understanding develops and to be able to relate this to specific lesson goals. Although teachers and, increasingly, pupils have become familiar with the language of national levels, it is important to remember that these are a reporting tool used to convey information about progress at set times in a pupil's school life. They do not have great value in supporting teachers in making day-to-day decisions about helping pupils to move on.

The role of the indicators or maps of progression in formative assessment is two-fold. First, as suggested earlier, the statements help focus the teacher's observation on significant aspects of behavior. Second, they help in interpreting the evidence that can come from pupils' talk, writing, drawing, and artifacts. By comparing this evidence with the indicators, teachers can gauge the point in development at which pupils are operating. Evidence from these sources can be used to compare with the indicators to see where in the progression the pupils seem to have reached. Finding where the answer is "yes, there is evidence of this" and where it is "no, there is no evidence of this"—or, more realistically, where it becomes difficult to say yes or no—locates the pupil's development within the progression. Furthermore, and crucially, this process indicates the next step, which is to consolidate the skills and ideas around the area where "yes" turns into "no." Finding where progress is to be made is the whole purpose of formative assessment.

HELPING PUPILS TO TAKE THE NEXT STEPS

There are two important ways for teachers to use the information from formative assessment: 1) to gain feedback into their own teaching, and 2) to give feedback to their pupils so that pupils also have information about where they are in relation to the goals of learning and know what to do to take the next steps.

Adjusting Teaching

Since the purpose of formative assessment is to guide decisions about how to help learning, the next steps for pupils cannot be planned in detail until the evidence is collected and interpreted. Although teachers' experience will enable them to be prepared for the kinds of ideas and skills that they are likely to find, the implementation of formative assessment allows for decisions to be taken on the basis of how pupils respond to their learning activities. However, the teacher can be prepared with strategies to use in various circumstances.

Strategies that are appropriate in science and mathematics include:

- extending experience, especially through materials to explore at first hand
- teaching new techniques, such as the conventions of drawing graphs, pie charts, and other representations of data, or the correct use of a microscope or measuring instrument
- enabling pupils to test and discuss their ideas so that they can dismiss their preconceived ideas and be more receptive to alternative, more scientific ideas

- providing access to alternative ideas, through discussion with peers or with "experts," and access to sources of information such as the internet, CD-ROMs and reference books
- providing challenging tasks while also providing support (scaffolding) so that pupils can experience operating at a more advanced level
- promoting dialogue, communication, and reflection

The last of these is widely acknowledged to be central to the process of learning and to formative assessment, both in yielding access to pupils' ideas, as noted earlier, and in facilitating progress (Black & Wiliam, 1998a, 1998b). Science and mathematics lessons provide many opportunities for talk about ideas, materials, and events. But there are many ways of "discussing" and using talk, so we need to be more specific about the kind of talk that helps in the development of pupils' thinking and capabilities. A great deal is included in the word *dialogue*. Its characteristics are described by Mercer, Dawes, Wegerif, and Sams (2004) as "exploratory," meaning that

- all relevant information is shared,
- all members of the group are invited to contribute to the discussion,
- opinions and ideas are respected and considered,
- everyone is asked to make their reasons clear,
- challenges and alternative are made explicit and are negotiated, and
- the group seeks to reach agreement before making a decision or acting. (p. 362)

In an investigation of how the use of this exploratory talk might impact pupils' learning in science, Mercer and colleagues developed a "Thinking Together" intervention program for teachers. This involved modeling and practicing talk with the above characteristics. In a controlled trial, the research showed that pupils who participated in the program improved their knowledge and understanding in science and their general reasoning skills significantly more than those without this experience (Asoko & Scott, 2006).

Alexander (2004) describes the use of this kind of talk as "a distinct pedagogical approach." He writes:

Dialogic teaching harnesses the power of talk to stimulate and extend children's thinking, and to advance their learning and understanding. It also enables the teacher more precisely to diagnose and assess. Dialogic teaching is distinct from the question-answer-tell routine of so-called "interactive" teaching, aiming to be more consistently searching and more genuinely reciprocal and cumulative. (p. 1)

As Alexander points out, the process of dialogic teaching is very similar to that of formative assessment. It aims to engage pupils and teachers in listening carefully and responding to each other, asking and answering questions, expressing and explaining and evaluating ideas, arguing and justifying. In this process, teachers can both gain and use information about how pupils' learning is progressing.

This involves the teacher, but pupil-only dialogue also has a very important role. For this to be successful, it is probably necessary for the teacher to "model" the supporting and reciprocal exchanges described by Mercer et al. (2004). When pupils can do this alone, there is an additional benefit, since "the teacher's absence removes from their work the usual source of authority; they cannot turn to him to solve dilemmas. Thus . . . the children not only formulate hypotheses, but are compelled to evaluate them for themselves" (Barnes, 1976, p. 29).

Providing Feedback to Pupils

The essence of formative assessment is that this evidence is used in adjusting teaching (see Wiliam & Leahy, Chapter 3, this volume), but an important opportunity for helping learning is missed if this is the only route for feedback into learning. At the very least, teachers should share with pupils their views on their work in such a way that the pupils understand the feedback and what it means in terms of what they need to do.

Feedback from their teacher is the means by which pupils find out how their work matches up to expectations and how far they have met intended goals. There is a good deal of research to show that feedback has a critical impact on motivation for learning, meaning the energy or drive to undertake further learning (Harlen & Deakin Crick, 2003; Brookhart, Chapter 4, this volume). Pupils are influenced by feedback from two main sources: their perceived success or failure in comparison with others in previous tasks that were similar to the one with which they are now faced, and the kind of feedback they receive from their teacher. Both of these depend on how teachers respond to pupils' work, whether through spoken comments or written feedback in the form of "marking" or "checking."

In relation to the content of the feedback, research by Butler (1988) on the effect of different kinds of feedback has been influential. She randomly assigned fifth and sixth grade pupils to groups that received different kinds of feedback. One group received grades on their work; the second received grades and comments; the third received comments only. Measures of achievement and of interest in undertaking further work were compared for these groups. It was found that when the pupils were working on tasks requiring divergent thinking, both high- and low-achieving pupils achieved more when given comments only than either grades or grades and comments. The interest in further work (motivation) of high achievers was the same for all feedback conditions, but low achievers expressed most interest after receiving comments only.

One reason for these results is that a grade or mark diverts pupils' attention from any comments, however useful they may be. The pupils focus on the grade, which is often seen as relating to "how good I am." This kind of feedback is described as judgmental or "ego-involving," rather than relating to the task and how to do it better. Grades are also backward-looking and do not indicate what now needs to be done—which is the intention in formative classroom assessment. Black et al. (2002) comment that "These results often surprise teachers, but those who have abandoned the giving of marks find that their experience confirms the findings: pupils do engage more productively in improving their work" (p. 8). They go on to report how teachers' concerns about possible adverse reactions from pupils, parents, and senior management—even school inspectors—to omitting grades when they give feedback proved to be unfounded. Comments given to pupils enabled both parents and pupils to focus on the learning to be done rather than on trying to interpret the meaning of a mark or grade. Some teachers who were required to assign marks because of school policy did this in their own record books but did not write them on pupils' work; others gave marks after the pupils had had a chance to respond to comments.

Other good teacher practices include focusing comments on the work, saying what is good about it as well as how it can be improved, avoiding superficial comments ("a good try"), and making sure that the comments reflect the goals of the work, not the spelling or tidiness, unless these were specified parts of the task. Finally, if comments require a response from the pupils, time has to be given for this.

In a research project that looked at pupils' perceptions of assessment and its place in their learning (LEARN Project, 1999), pupils had many comments to make about the effect of feedback from their teachers. These comments illustrate the value of different approaches. A few examples include the following:

If it's a tick I'm quite happy because it means it's good work, but if it's two sentences at the bottom it means it's quite bad. (Year 6, age 11, pupil)

Some teachers put things you could work on to make it better. I like that 'cos you can work on it more. (Year 9, age 14, pupil)

What the teacher says is most important because it's one on one so they can tell you what they really think. (Year 9, age 14, pupil)

That's a 5. I don't know what it means. I've got it on some of my work. I think it's a grade thing. (Year 10, age 15, pupil)

Good doesn't help much—he's just saying that it's not really very good. I'd like it if he just told the truth. (Year 3, age 8, pupil)

Not very good work . . . doesn't help me know how to do it better. (Year 3, age 8, pupil).

(pp. 12–14)

Involving Pupils in Formative Assessment

There are both sound theoretical and practical reasons for involving pupils in the formative assessment of their work. The theory relates to the view of learning outlined briefly at the start of this chapter, in which learners are at the center of the process. It follows that the more learners know about what it is intended that they should learn—the learning goals, about where they are in relation to these goals, and about what further needs to be done to reach the goals—the more they can direct their efforts usefully for learning. Other arguments (e.g., Boud, 1995, 2000; Sadler, 1998) refer to the development of capacity for lifelong learning and to the development of autonomy (Marshall in this volume). Furthermore, there is research showing that self-assessment can raise levels of achievement (Delclos & Harrington, 1991; Fontana & Fernandes, 1994; Frederiksen & White, 1997; Schunk, 1996; Stiggins, Chapter 2, this volume).

Teachers who practice pupil self- and peer-assessment maintain that it enables pupils to take ownership of their learning and see themselves as partners in the teaching-learning process, raising their self-esteem. It helps them to question and refine their own concepts, and to become more self-critical and proactive as learners. They see assessment as a process in which they are involved and to which they can make a contribution, and they see that they are setting the next target, rather than having the target externally imposed (Harlen & Qualter, 2004).

Teachers introducing self-assessment for the first time may encounter resistance from pupils. In the LEARN Project research (1999), pupils said that they did not feel it was part of their "role" to assess their own work. They had a clear view that this was the teachers' job and they did not feel that they knew how to tackle it. Older pupils could more clearly see some value in this practice. Here are some of their comments:

> Once in maths I ticked my own work. It's not good to mark your own work because you don't know if it's right or wrong. (Year 3, age 8, pupil)

> In English we have a partner and you swap books and you assess them and the teacher takes them in. I don't like that really. It's better if the teacher does it really. (Year 9, age 14, pupil)

> In Geography we had an essay and he said to try to pick out the mistakes and give it a mark out of twenty. It was good to see what kind of mistakes we made. (Year 10, age 15, pupil)

> (pp. 10–11)

These comments indicate a persistent view of assessment as being about making judgments rather than helping learning. However, Black and Harrison (2004) recount how coaching, using criteria and modeling, enables pupils to gradually assimilate feedback from self- and peer-assessment into their view of what is quality work. They point out, "This is clearly enhanced if the pupils are also regularly receiving effective guidance comments from their teachers as this provides the language, style and model to help them discuss their work with one another and provide feedback" (p. 16).

Communicating Goals and Quality Criteria

In science and mathematics, learning goals generally include the development of inquiry skills. These are much less obvious to pupils than are goals that relate to the science knowledge content or to the subject matter of mathematical "problems." The result may be that pupils focus on what is rather trivial in relation to content rather than on the process of inquiry. This happened in a science class where some year 7 (12-year-old) boys spent three lessons finding out which of three kinds of paper was the strongest. After the lesson, an observer interviewed the boys:

> *Interviewer:* What do you think you have learned from doing your
>   investigations?
> *Robert:* That graph paper is strongest, that green one.
> *Interviewer:* Right, is that it?
> *Robert:* Um. . . .
> *Interviewer:* You spent three lessons doing that, seems a long time to
>   spend finding out that graph paper is stronger.
> *James:* Yeah, and we also found which . . . papers is [sic] stronger.
>   Not just the graph paper, all of them.

As summarized by Harlen (2001),

> The boys appeared to be unaware of the process of investigation as a learn-
> ing goal, in contrast with their teacher. It seems reasonable to assume that,
> had they been aware of this goal, they would have reflected more on the way
> they were investigating, found more satisfaction in the investigation, and made
> more progress toward the goal that the teacher had in mind but kept to her-
> self. (p. 132)

Communicating goals related to the process of learning and assuring a shared understanding of these goals is not easy because it is not the same as simply indicating what the pupils should be learning (for instance, that wood is a better insulator than metal). Rather, it is explaining what they will be learning *about* (whether some materials are better insulators than others) and *how* they will be learning (testing the materials so that they can be sure that they are making a fair comparison). Examples of the practice of sharing goals in science are given by Goldsworthy, Watson, and Wood-Robinson (2000), who point out the value of teachers' checking what their pupils think are the aims of a lesson. This can be done informally by asking pupils why they think they have been asked to carry out a particular activity, or more formally, by occasionally asking pupils to write down, toward the end of a lesson, what they think their teacher wants them to learn in this lesson. Then the teacher can study the responses in depth and compare them with the intended aims of the lesson.

Some teachers use examples of work to convey the meaning of quality criteria, using some that do and some that do not meet the criteria. Another approach is to make the criteria explicit in assigning work, using words such as "What I'm looking for in your plan is. . . ." However, the problem of conveying the meaning of the criteria is lessened if pupils help to identify them. In science, teachers sometimes do this by holding a class discussion to brainstorm with pupils what is expected in a "good" plan or a "good" report of an investigation, or in a satisfactory explanation. At the same time, the teacher can take the opportunity to add some criteria with the agreement of the pupils (e.g., the lessons described by Marshall, Chapter 9 in this volume). Following one such discussion, the teacher wrote the list in large print on a chart and pinned it to the wall. While the pupils wrote reports of their investigation, they were reminded to pay attention to the points listed. When they presented their reports to each other, they used the list to make constructive comments about how the reports (both their own and others') could be improved.

An approach to self-assessment used by teachers of younger pupils is to ask pupils at the end of a piece or unit of work to look at what they have done and try to answer three questions:

- What have I done well?
- What could I have done better?
- What do I need to do to improve?

When this is first done, it is necessary for the teacher to sit down with pupils individually to discuss the answers. In these discussions, the teacher can make sure that the pupils are making realistic judgments of their work and, if necessary, can inject some criteria related to the learning goals.

For older pupils, a practice growing in popularity is the "traffic light approach." Here, pupils have a supply of green, yellow, and red self-adhesive spots (traffic lights). As they complete their work, before handing it in to the teacher, they indicate their own understanding of it by using one of the spots. They stick on a green spot when they are confident of their understanding, a yellow one if they are not totally confident, and a red one if they do not understand something about it. The teacher then knows at a glance whether, in the next lesson, he or she should revisit some of this work for all the pupils, or proceed to new work while making sure to discuss the material with a few pupils to clear up misunderstandings. Some variants on this approach are reported by Black et al. (2002). They also found that peer assessment has an important role in pupils' learning:

> Peer assessment is uniquely valuable because pupils may accept from one another, criticisms of their work, which they would not take seriously if made by their teacher. Peer work is also valuable because the interchange will be in a language that pupils themselves would naturally use and because pupils learn by taking the roles of teachers and examiners of others. (Sadler, 1998, cited in Black et al., 2002, p. 10)

Moreover, having pupils talk to each other about their work requires them to think through the work again and perhaps explain or justify it without the pressure that comes from the unequal relationship between pupil (novice) and teacher (expert). It is also consistent with learning through social interaction, as well as through interaction with materials. Further, peer assessment helps pupils to recognize each other's strengths, and sets up situations where they can help each other (e.g. Rea-Dickins, 2001). It does, of course, require a classroom ethos of cooperation and collaboration rather than competition, but this is a prerequisite for a good deal of the features of classroom assessment discussed here.

MANAGING FORMATIVE ASSESSMENT

However persuasive the arguments and research evidence for formative assessment, change in practice can present a formidable challenge. Concern often focuses on the supposed need to give pupils individual attention when there are many in the class. Teachers also worry about how often they should be conducting formative assessment, and which activities to choose. Some of these concerns indicate the persistence of a view that formative assessment is an addition to teaching, rather than an integral part of it. Other concerns disappear when teachers realize that using assessment formatively creates greater pupil self-direction and responsibility for pupils' own learning. When this is achieved, teachers have more time to spend with those who need more help to reach this point.

As part of teaching, formative assessment should be included in all lesson plans. The starting point in planning is to consider the goals of the work. If these involve the development of ideas related to particular content, then the teacher must use methods of gathering and using information for all the pupils while they are engaged with this content. For the development of inquiry skills, on the other hand, there will be many activities involving the skills in relation to different subject matter, so the information can be gathered and used over a period of time, focusing on the particular skills that an activity involves.

When information is being gathered by observation, the teacher can focus on one group at a time. This does not mean neglecting other groups, just that in interaction with the "target" group, the teacher will question, probe, and observe with specific indicators in mind. It may take several weeks to cover all the pupils in this way, and it will mean that different pupils are observed when they are carrying out different activities. This is not a problem in the context of formative assessment, since the purpose is not to assign a grade or label but to help pupils' use of inquiry skills in the particular activities they encounter.

Pupils will often be working in groups, and teachers generally have no difficulty in identifying the separate contributions of pupils even when they are combining their ideas and skills in a group enterprise. However, for the purpose of formative assessment, it is not always necessary to assess individual pupils. If the information is used to make decisions about the activities and help is given to pupils *as a group*, then assessment of the group is all that is needed for this purpose. In group work, differences between pupils are not a disadvantage, since there is convincing evidence that in heterogeneous groups all pupils benefit when they are encouraged to share ideas and skills (Howe, Rodgers, & Tolmic, 1992; Topping & Thurston, 2004). Thus, a group assessment may be all that is necessary where the activity is genuinely collaborative and ideas are pooled. Evidence of the achievements of individuals can be found in the products of their work and discussion of these products.

BARRIERS TO IMPLEMENTING FORMATIVE ASSESSMENT

With so many good reasons for implementing effective classroom assessment, the question arises as to why its practice is not already widespread. There are several answers to this question, which have been brought together in a series of pamphlets by the Assessment Reform Group (ARG) (see www .assessment-reform-group.org). The primary barriers were: 1) existing assessment practices that give more attention to grading and assigning pupils to proficiency levels, rather than to giving feedback about how work could be improved; 2) the lack of awareness among teachers about pupils' learning needs; and 3) the high stakes attached to national or statewide test results, which encourage teachers to focus on the content of the tests and practicing test-taking.

An important source of difficulty in the widespread implementation of summative assessment is often presented as a conflict between formative and summative assessment. I maintain that both are needed for different purposes in education and can exist, in theory, in synergy (Harlen, 2005). In practice, however, summative assessment dominates when pupil test results are used for purposes other than decisions about individual pupils. In particular, the use of test results as the sole data for evaluation of the performance of teachers and schools is responsible for the high stakes that drive teachers to an over-use of transmission teaching and highly structured activities. This conflicts with what is needed for pupils to enjoy and be motivated to learn science and mathematics (ARG, 2006).

Bringing about change in teachers is notoriously difficult (Fullan, 2003), particularly when it demands the quite fundamental change in pedagogy that implementing formative assessment requires of many teachers. Reflecting on their work with teachers, Black et al. (2002) note that there is

> an element of risk involved for both teachers and pupils and both . . . have to work harder, at least to begin with. Teachers taking on formative assessment are giving their pupils a voice and in many cases acting so as to make that voice louder. For many teachers that is a difficult road. . . . Making changes in prac-tice can make a confident teacher feel incompetent. They are setting up an unfamiliar classroom culture and both teacher and pupils may feel insecure at the start. (pp. 98, 99)

The same authors report, however, on the changes taking place in teach-ers with whom they worked for an extended time and who changed not only their practice but their beliefs about how pupils learn. As they began to give pupils more control over their learning, they found a sense of enjoyment and confidence in teaching that was matched by the pupils' greater confidence and enjoyment in learning.

CONCLUSIONS

Implementing formative assessment has implications for all aspects of teach-ing practice and may require some quite fundamental changes when first adopted. Introducing formative assessment is not simply a matter of add-ing some new procedures, but of creating a classroom ethos in which pupils and teachers share responsibility for using assessment to help learn-ing. It is a matter of valuing learning and teaching in ways that achieve particular outcomes. Thus, the actions needed to implement formative as-sessment in science and mathematics, discussed and illustrated in this chap-ter, have to be seen in the context of the purpose and reasons for these practices.

The overall purpose is to foster learning with understanding and the skills and attitudes that are needed for successful and continued learning. Both domain-specific and more general learning goals are involved. In relation to science and mathematics, the aims are best expressed in terms of scientific and mathematical literacy, the capacity to understand the role that science and mathematics take in everyday life and to use scientific and mathematical knowledge in different context to make decisions "as a constructive, concerned and reflective citizen" (Organisation for Economic Co-operation and Development [OECD], 1999, p. 41). The more general goals are to be able to "organise and regulate their own learning, to learn independently and in groups, and to overcome difficulties in the learning process. This requires them to be aware of their own thinking processes and learning strategies and methods" (pp. 9–10).

Formative assessment helps in the achievement of these aims because it involves both teacher and pupils in being clear about learning goals, about where pupils are in relation to them, and about taking decisions regarding further steps that need to be taken. It means that teachers require an understanding of overall goals and how individual lesson goals relate to them. They not only need to be able to identify where pupils are, but also to help pupils do this for themselves.

This chapter has emphasized that "where pupils are" refers to their status in relation to progress in the development of skills and understanding, not in relation to "levels" or "standards" that describe and are often used as a measure of summative achievement. Summative assessment serves a quite different purpose from formative assessment. It is necessary for reporting on progress at certain times and, although in some circumstances it can have some formative function (Black, Harrison, Lee, Marshall, & Wiliam, 2003), its necessarily summative nature makes it unsuitable for this purpose. Formative assessment is concerned with working toward detailed goals of an individual lesson or groups of lessons on a topic. It is possible, and for many reasons desirable, to review evidence gathered and used for formative assessment and to assess it against the broad summative criteria for reporting progress (Harlen, in press). However, it is important that this is a holistic review, a reinterpretation of the evidence gathered during learning, not a summation of judgments. Otherwise, formative assessment becomes a series of mini-summative judgments, with a focus on easily assessed surface learning and a subsequent reduction of opportunities for achieving learning of the kind discussed here.

REFERENCES

Alexander, R. (2004). *Towards dialogic teaching: Rethinking classroom talk*. Cambridge, UK: Dialogos.

ARG (Assessment Reform Group). (2006). *The role of teachers in the assessment of learning*. London: Author.

Asoko, H., & Scott, P. (2006). Talk in science classrooms. In W. Harlen (Ed.), *ASE guide to primary science education.* Hatfield, UK: Association for Science Education.

Association for Science Education (ASE). (2002). *ASE science year primary CD ROM.* Hatfield, UK: ASE.

Barnes, D. (1976). *From communication to curriculum.* Harmondsworth, UK: Penguin.

Black, P., & Harrison, C. (2004). *Science inside the black box.* London: NFER-Nelson.

Black, P., Harrison, C., Lee, C., Marshall, B., & Wiliam, D. (2002). *Working inside the black box: Assessment for learning in the classroom.* London: King's College.

Black, P., Harrison, C., Lee, C., Marshall, B., & Wiliam, D. (2003). *Assessment for learning: Putting it into practice.* Maidenhead, UK: Open University.

Black, P., & Wiliam, D. (1998a). Assessment and classroom learning. *Assessment in Education, 5,* 1–74.

Black, P., & Wiliam D. (1998b). *Inside the black box: Raising standards through classroom assessment.* London: School of Education, King's College.

Boud, D. (1995). *Enhancing learning through self assessment.* London: Kogan Page.

Boud, D. (2000). Sustainable assessment: Rethinking assessment for the learning society. *Studies in Continuing Education, 22*(2), 151–167.

Butler, R. (1988). Enhancing and undermining intrinsic motivation: The effects of task-involving and ego-involving evaluation on interest and performance. *British Journal of Educational Psychology, 58,* 1–14.

Delclos, V. R., & Harrington, C. (1991). Effects of strategy monitoring and proactive instruction on children's problem-solving performance. *Journal of Educational Psychology, 83,* 35–42.

Department for Education and Skills (DfES)/Qualifications and curriculum authority (QCA). (1999). *The national curriculum: Handbook for secondary teachers in England.* London: HMSO/QCA.

Driver, R., & Scott, P. (1995). Mind in communication: A response to Erick Smith. *Educational Researcher, 23* (7) 27–28.

Fontana, D., & Fernandes, M. (1994). Improvements in mathematics performance as a consequence of self-assessment in Portuguese primary school pupils. *British Journal of Educational Psychology, 64,* 407–417.

Frederiksen, J. R., & White, B. J. (1997, April). *Reflective assessment of pupils' research within an inquiry-based middle school curriculum.* Paper presented at the Annual Meeting of the American Educational Research Association, Chicago.

Fullan, M. (2003). *Change forces with a vengeance.* London: Routledge Falmer.

Goldsworthy, A., Watson, R., & Wood-Robinson, V. (2000). *Investigations: Targeted learning.* Hatfield: ASE.

Harlen, W. (2001). *Primary science: Taking the plunge* (2nd Ed.). Portsmouth, NH: Heinemann.

Harlen, W. (2005). Teachers' summative practices and assessment for learning—tensions and synergies. *The Curriculum Journal, 16*(2), 207–223.

Harlen, W. (2006). *Teaching, learning and assessing science 5–12* (4th Ed.). London: Sage.

Harlen, W. (in press). Trusting teachers' judgement. In S. Swaffield (ed.), *Unlocking assessment.* London: David Fulton.

Harlen, W., & Deakin Crick, R. (2003). Testing and motivation for learning. *Assessment in Education, 10*(2), 169–208.

Harlen, W., & James, M. (1997). Assessment and learning: Difference and relationships between formative and summative assessment. *Assessment in Education, 4*, 365–380.

Harlen, W., & Qualter, A. (2004). *The teaching of science in primary schools.* London: David Fulton Publishers.

Howe, C. J., Rodgers, C., & Tolmic, A. (1992). The acquisition of conceptual understanding of science in primary school children: Group interaction and the understanding of motion down an incline. *British Journal of Developmental Psychology, 10*, 113–130.

Institute for Inquiry. (2003). *Enhancing inquiry through formative assessment.* San Francisco: The Exploratorium.

Keogh, B., & Naylor, S. (2000). *Concept cartoons in science education.* Sandbach, Cheshire: Millgate House Publishers.

LEARN Project. (1999). Report for QCA published on the QCA Web site at http://www.qca.org.uk/ages3–14/afl/292.html

Masters, G., & Forster, M. (1996). *Progress maps.* Camberwell, Victoria: Australian Council for Research in Education.

Mercer, N., Dawes, L., Wegerif, R., & Sams, C. (2004). Reasoning as a scientist: Ways of helping children to use language to learn science. *British Educational Research Journal, 30*(3), 359–377.

National Research Council (NRC). (1995). *National science education standards.* Washington, DC: National Academy Press.

Novak, J. D., & Gowan, D. B. (1984). *Learning how to learn.* London: Cambridge University Press.

Organisation for Economic Cooperation and Development (OECD). (1999). *Measuring pupil knowledge and skills. A new framework for assessment.* Paris: Author.

Qualifications and Curriculum Authority (QCA). (2001). *Using assessment to raise achievement in mathematics. Key stages 1, 2 and 3.* Published on QCA Web site at http://www.qca.org.uk/ca/5–14/afl/

Rea-Dickins, P. (2001). Mirror, mirror on the wall: Identifying process of classroom assessment. *Language Testing, 18*, 429–462.

Rowe, M. B. (1974). Wait time and rewards as instructional variables, their influence on language, logic and fate control. *Journal of Research in Science Teaching, 11*, 81–94.

Sadler, R. (1998). Formative assessment: Revisiting the territory. *Assessment in Education, 5*(1), 77–84.

Schunk, D. H. (1996). Goal and self-evaluation influences during children's cognitive skill learning. *American Educational Research Journal, 33*, 359–382.

Topping, K. J., & Thurston, A. (2004). *Enjoying science together.* Grangemouth, Scotland, UK: Geoquest/British Petroleum.

Watson, A., & Mason, J. (1998). *Questions and prompts for mathematical thinking.* Derby: Association of Teachers of Mathematics.

Wilson, M., Kennedy, C., & Draney, K. (2004). *GradeMap* (Version 4.0) (Computer Program). Berkeley, CA: University of California, BEAR Center.

CHAPTER 9

Formative Classroom Assessment in English, the Humanities, and Social Sciences

Bethan Marshall

Much of the literature on formative assessment, or assessment *for* learning (AfL), has arisen out of work in math and science. This is possibly because the constructivist view of learning in these disciplines lends itself to very clear paths of progression (see Harlen, Chapter 8, this volume) onto which formative assessment can be readily mapped. Work of a similar nature does not exist in English and the humanities or in the social sciences, where progression is a much messier business. It is hard, for example, in English to be precise about the developmental trajectory of the imagination. Nor is it easy, in history, to identify what role maturity plays in helping students extend their understanding from the personal to the abstract, to see the principle within the particular.

Part of the explanation may lie in the way the disciplines have been conceived, both traditionally and currently. Although there has been much vigorous, and on occasion acrimonious, debate within English and the humanities about the balance between content knowledge and process knowhow, most recent views of these subjects have erred toward the latter view (see, for example, Hayden, 2004; Lambert, 2004; and Marshall, 2000). The process-orientated curriculum is organized around broad generic concepts and skills to which content can be multifariously applied from an early age. This iterative process, between content and process, enables children to explore their place within the world and critique the formation of the society in which they live.

Unlike math and science, which has developed a specific predetermined sequence for the teaching of certain concepts, in English, the humanities, and social science, progression becomes a more meandering, organic affair. Children encounter, for example, the idea of chronology from the very beginning of school history and then revisit this basic idea, in various forms and contexts, from then on, each time deepening their understanding. Geography, similarly, has several big ideas, such as interdependence or sustainability, and a larger number of key concepts, such as "friction of distance," "erosion," and "deposition." All of these build into what some are now calling "geographical literacy" with which students engage from the start (Weelden & Lambert, 2006). And while people may nuance the subject of English in particular ways, many, if not most, agree that English is about the art of language, though the importance of technical acumen and an ability to convey meaning are, of course, also essential elements. This aesthetic dimension distinguishes English from both literacy and communication studies in that it emphasizes the imaginative and creative scope of the subject—the possibility of forming ideas into words. As a core activity, however, it differs little in essence whether one is 5 or 55. All that potentially changes is the complexity and sophistication of the texts consumed and produced.

UNDERPINNING PRINCIPLES

Student Engagement

One way of understanding progression in English, the humanities, and social science, then, is to see it as aiming toward a horizon rather than a specific goal (see Marshall, 2004a, 2004b, 2004c), in which talk, debate, and reflection are essential pedagogic tools in the development of these central ideas and processes. This lends itself well to the first principle of formative assessment—the student is engaged in the process. Perhaps this is why many teachers of English and humanities would recognize the strategies advocated as "formative" as best practice within their discipline. Black and Wiliam (1998) defined *formative assessment* as:

> All those activities undertaken by teachers, *and by their students in assessing themselves*, which provide information to be used as feedback to modify the teaching and learning activities in which they are engaged. *Such assessment becomes "formative assessment" when the evidence is actually used to adapt the teaching work to meet the needs.* (p. 2; emphasis in original)

Students as Independent Learners

This principle sits alongside what might be considered the main aim of formative assessment—that students become independent learners. In this way, the strategies advocated to encourage formative assessment act like a kind of "Trojan horse" (see Black, McCormick, James, & Pedder, 2006) by which the AfL procedures bring about a progressive pedagogy. The four dominant strategies or procedures that emerged from the research, undertaken during the King's Medway Oxfordshire Formative Assessment Project (KMOFAP), as the main means by which teachers might implement formative assessment in their classroom were:

- classroom talk, including the role of questioning and other activities that promote talk
- feedback
- sharing learning intentions and success criteria with the learner
- peer and self-assessment

Although each can be considered discretely, all overlap. How can students assess themselves or their peers without understanding the criteria? How can feedback be meaningful unless the task is appropriate? More importantly, students need to be understood in the context of the broader aim of AfL rather than as ends in themselves. The work of both Vygotsky and Dewey is helpful here. Crucial to appreciating the relevance, for formative assessment, of Vygotsky and Dewey's understanding of learning is the notion of progression toward autonomy and the teachers' role in facilitating this through the activities in which they encourage students to engage.

Most obvious is Vygotsky's concept of the zone of proximal development (ZPD) (Vygotsky, 1978)—what a child can do with support today, he or she can do alone tomorrow. But significant, also, is Dewey's (1966) definition of *progressive education* as "high organization based upon ideas" (pp. 28–29). The challenge is "to discover and put into operation a principle of order and operation which follows from understanding what the educative experience signifies" (p. 29). Dewey acknowledges that it is "a difficult task to work out the kinds of materials, of methods, and of social relationships that are appropriate" (p. 29). In a sense, this is what the application of formative assessment asks teachers to attempt. The implementation of AfL in the classroom, then, comes to be about much more than the application of certain procedures—questioning, feedback, sharing the criteria with the learner, and peer and self-assessment. It is about the realization of certain principles of teaching and learning.

Student Communication

Two other guiding principles aid this process. The first is that talk is an aid to learning. Again, this has long been deemed good practice in English and humanities and builds on the work of Vygotsky and Bruner (1963). Within the ZPD, they suggested, students need to interact with those who are "more capable." This interaction with peers and teachers provides a "scaffolding" for the learner, through which learners develop the capabilities themselves.

On a more practical level, teachers are involved in carefully devising and creating tasks that maximize opportunities for students to think through and develop their ideas as an aid to understanding and writing. The richer the task, the more meaningful the teachers' feedback. Within this model of teaching and learning, the most frequent form of feedback will be oral—characteristically, based on the research evidence of KMOFAP, a follow-up question that prompts further thinking.

Guild Knowledge: Peer and Self-Assessment

More particularly, within English and the humanities, students need to be apprenticed into what Royce Sadler (1989) describes as "guild knowledge." This means that they need to learn to develop judgment about the quality of work they and others produce in relation to the core concepts and processes of the subject. Significantly, Sadler suggests that simply providing lists of criteria for what makes a piece of writing or performance good is insufficient in helping students to progress for three reasons:

- The whole is always more than the sum of its constituent parts.
- The interrelationship between all the constituent components is always too complex to be meaningfully itemized.
- The diversity of potential outcomes makes the use of criteria too restrictive to be helpful in suggesting progression.

Instead, Sadler (1989) argues that students need to be apprenticed into the guild through the assessment process. Dylan Wiliam (2000) has suggested that UK English teachers, for example, develop—principally through assessing students' work and through attending standardizing meetings—a shared construct of what a particular grade looks like. Observation of these standardization meetings illustrates the point (see Marshall, 2000). In these meetings, the use of criteria is always subordinate to the teacher's overall impression of the quality of the candidates' work. In one exchange, for example, a moderator rejected the idea that the grade should be determined from a simplistic assessment against analytic criteria because "This screams D at me." What is vital to the process is the way in which the teachers learn to interpret the evidence.

Peer and self-assessment enables students to begin the development of a similar understanding of the construct that the community of teachers already shares. Discussion about their own writing and that of others enables them to gain insight into what is involved in, for example, a good essay, and thus apprentices students into the guild. In so doing, it extends the range and scope of their repertoire by helping them see what quality looks like.

None of these principles matters, however, unless it is realized that the relationship between the teacher and student is crucial in developing a formative assessment classroom. As Black and Wiliam (1998) observe, it is "the quality of the interaction [between student and teacher] which is at the heart of pedagogy" (p. 16). There is, in the end, no substitute for the teacher's actually being interested in what the students have to say. At the heart of all true dialogue lies the relationship between the participants.

PRINCIPLES IN PRACTICE

Two English Lessons

One way of understanding how formative assessment strategies work in the classroom, the way these strategies inevitably overlap, and their potential to promote independent learning is to compare two lessons in some detail. The categories used in Figure 9.1, "Letter" and "Spirit," which arise out of research undertaken in England over a four-year period, are designed to capture the difference in the application of these strategies (see Marshall & Drummond, 2006). Tracy and Angela were both teachers on the project. The lessons under discussion were videoed as part of the research to better understand how teachers were implementing AfL strategies. Both teachers were filmed, often having been informed that this was the purpose of the visit. Figure 9.1 gives a brief outline of the main activities within each lesson. A change in activity is marked by a bullet.

On the surface, the lessons share much in common. Like many English lessons, they were designed to engage students both with the content of the subject—in this case pre-20th-century texts—and their own performance in English through a related creative task. In one lesson, this took the form of a piece of writing; in the other, speaking and listening. In Tracy's lesson, the students had written a letter in the voice of one of the characters in the text for homework and were using this lesson as an opportunity to improve their work. In Angela's lesson, the students had read the poem in the previous lesson and were now being asked to perform a section of it.

Both lessons had the potential for students to engage with the question of what makes for quality in a piece of work—an issue that is difficult in English and hard for students to grasp (Marshall, 2004c, 2006). Both Tracy and Angela overtly adopted two of the procedures of formative assessment identified at the start of this chapter—sharing the criteria with the learner and peer and self-assessment—as a means to this end (although, as we shall

Figure 9.1. Student Activities in Two English Lessons

Letter (Tracy)	Spirit (Angela)
Year 8 Lesson A—Pre-20th Century Short Story	*Year 8 Lesson B—Pre-20th Century Poem*
• Tracy models criteria by sampling examples from the text she wishes students to correct	• Class draws up list of criteria, guided by teacher
• Students correct text	• Angela and LSA perform poem
• Tracy checks answers with whole class	• Students are asked to critique performance
• Students correct each other's work	• Students rehearse their own performance
	• Students assess peers based on criteria
	• Students perform poems based on criteria

see, feedback and dialogue are also crucial in the outworking of the formative nature of the lesson). These two activities—modeling and peer assessment—are linked. In both lessons, the modeling activity at the start of the lesson appears to have been designed to help students know what to do when they assess their peers. Indeed, this is one of the most common ways in which English teachers elicit or share criteria. A "model," or example of a piece of work, is used at the start of a lesson to illustrate what will subsequently be required of the students themselves at another point in the lesson.

Tracy's Short-Story Lesson

Tracy modeled the criteria for the eventual peer-assessment activity by giving students a piece of writing that was full of technical errors (i.e., spelling and punctuation). The students were asked to correct it on their own while Tracy went around the class monitoring their progress. The discourse revolved around notions of correctness, and there was little scope for anything other than closed questions. The second activity in Tracy's lesson again centered on the teacher checking whether or not the students had found the errors in the text. The whole-class feedback involved students volunteering to share where they had found a mistake and the correction they had made. Occasionally they missed something in the text and Tracy would go back until a student identified the missing error and corrected it. Similarly, on the small number of occasions when a student got the answer wrong, Tracy would pause, waiting for another student to volunteer the right answer. In this exchange, the teacher adjudicated all questions of correctness with no opportunity for the students to extend the narrowly defined scope of the task. Students then went on to assess each other's work.

Angela's Poem Lesson

Angela modeled the criteria for peer assessment differently, concentrating attention on issues related to quality. She began the lesson by asking the students to draw up a list of criteria for performing a poem. All suggestions came from the students. The exchanges were more open and provided more opportunity for the students' answers to be probed, extending their understanding of what makes for a good performance. The students were, to an extent, setting the agenda. They were being asked to propose criteria for success, and, through this, being drawn into questions of quality and judgment, which are arguably core activities in English. Angela did not abdicate responsibility. She subtly guided students' responses. Through interaction she also developed the students' critical vocabulary as the students' contributions were negotiated with the teacher who, through the exchange, refined them. For example:

> *Student:* You could speed it up and slow it down.
> *Angela:* Yes—pace, that's very important in reading.
> [Teacher then writes the word *pace* on the board.]

Angela and the classroom assistant then performed the poem for the class and invited students to critique their performance based on the criteria they had created. In so doing, they drew not just on the criteria but also on their interpretation of the poem. In this way, the dual nature of the lesson— developing the students' understanding of the literature and of speaking and listening—was also served. A similar form of probing took place in these exchanges as well. Angela used questions as a form of oral feedback in order to challenge and extend the students' responses:

> *Student:* It [the performance] was boring.
> *Angela:* What do you mean *boring*?
> *Student:* There wasn't enough expression in your face when the poem was being read or in the reading.
> *Angela:* So what could I have done to make it better?
> *Student:* You could have looked and sounded more alarmed.
> *Angela:* Like this? [Strikes a pose.]
> *Student:* Not quite.
> *Angela:* More like this? [Strikes another pose.]
> *Student:* Yeah.

These three tasks in Angela's lesson—the creation of the criteria, the performance of the poem, and the application of the criteria to Angela's and the assistant's performance—governed both the students' thinking about what was needed when they acted out the poem themselves and the peer assessment of those performances.

Lesson Differences

Two crucial but subtle elements differentiate these lessons: the potential scope of the tasks and the opportunities they afforded for current and future student independence. The scope of the task in Tracy's lesson was considerably more restricted in helping students understand what quality might look like, focusing instead on those things that were simply right and wrong. Students in Angela's lesson, on the other hand, engaged both in technical considerations, such as clarity and accuracy, as well as in the higher-order, interpretive concepts of meaning and effect. In addition, the modeling of what was required in Angela's lesson ensured that students went beyond an imitation of that model because it challenged them to think about the variety of ways in which they might enact their interpretation of the poem.

This also affected the type of talk between the students. The way in which the activities were initially framed contributed to the quality of student discussion. In Tracy's lesson, the correcting of the text was undertaken in almost complete silence, as was the peer assessment. The way in which the scope of the peer assessment had been defined by the previous task—largely a proofreading exercise—meant that there was no opportunity for them to discuss what they thought of the letters or how they might be improved, except in terms of spelling, punctuation, and grammar.

Students in Angela's lesson, on the other hand, were involved in a lively, extended discussion, first on how to render their section of the poem dramatically and then in critiquing the performance of their peers. In so doing, they too built on their understanding of the scope of the task as established by the previous activities. Each performance was the result of collaboration between the students in which, as they had done in the previous two activities, they extended their own understanding through the contributions and ideas of their peers. That they understood the task of performing the poem to be open-ended was evident in the wide variety of interpretations. That they understood how to make judgments as to quality in order to improve performance was demonstrated through the comments they made to their peers.

In this way, the sequence of activities guided the students in Angela's lesson toward being independent or autonomous learners. This was because the tasks, such as encouraging the students to create their own criteria, helped them to think for themselves about what might be needed to capture the meaning of the poem in performance. Students in Angela's lesson, therefore, also began to engage in the more complex issues of any performance, be it oral or written. Each stage of the lesson offered students an opportunity to refine and test their understanding of what was required through criticism and creative activity. Through the activities, students were asked to explore the relationship between the meaning of a product and the way in which that meaning is expressed: between form and content.

Moreover, Angela always described the tasks as opportunities for the students to improve their performance. In this way, the activities had an open, fluid feel that corresponded with the notion of promoting student autonomy; it reinforced a sense of limitless progress whereby assessment is always seen as a tool for future, rather than past, performance. Mainly this was done by creating tasks designed to enable children to enter the subject community or "guild" (Sadler, 1989). By contrast, in Tracy's lesson, the formative procedures alone were insufficient to lead to this key beneficial outcome of Angela's lesson. Performance in Tracy's lesson comprised a finite act, conforming to a fixed, identifiable, measurable notion of correctness in which issues of quality were not discussed.

History Lesson

In some respects, Angela's lesson represents Dewey's organization based on ideas as a means of understanding formative assessment in the classroom. To explore this idea further, we will now look at a history lesson taught to a mixed group of 12- to 13-year-olds. The lesson illustrates the importance of rich tasks, which develop the students' thinking as a vehicle toward independence, both through the nature of the tasks themselves and through the way in which they are sequenced. As with Angela's lesson, progression is brought about within the task through dialogue and between tasks—one arising out of the other, and so building on the previous one. David, the history teacher, used questioning and feedback as the most prominent formative procedures or strategies throughout the lesson to extend the students' historical understanding and skills.

The main curriculum content of the lesson was concerned with the slave trade triangle of the late 18th and early 19th centuries between England, Africa, and the Caribbean but, as with the English lesson, certain core concepts and key skills were also being taught, which apprenticed students into the subject community. In this instance, students were asked to consider what type of evidence certain sources might proffer, how to use such sources, and what the role of chronology was. Toward the end of the lesson, they also began to consider the type of language and register necessary for writing about historical sources.

The lesson was divided into three main activities, each building on the other, to achieve David's broad stated aim, which was to "deepen their [the students'] understanding of how the slave trade operated" and how to use sources to do so. This dual aim was clearly articulated in the learning outcomes David placed on the overhead projector at the start of the lesson. He told the students that by the end of the hour they would "be able to explain how the slave trade operated and demonstrate this by sequencing, categorizing and inference from visual sources."

Review of Learning from Previous Lesson

The first activity recapped what students had learned in previous lessons. This could have been done by simply asking students to list the main "facts" they had learned the day before. Instead, David asked five multiple-choice questions pertaining to the slave trade, and students had to identify the odd answer out in a list of four. Each question contained information that students would need to be reminded of for the next stage of the lesson, but what was important was less the answer than how they justified their ideas, an aim David pointed out on a number of occasions during this section of the lesson.

The preeminence of justification as an aim was most evident in an exchange on the question that listed factory workers, construction workers, servants, and farmworkers. The students displayed their answers simultaneously on small white boards so that David could, at a glance, see the range of responses. The students were divided in their answers between the first two. It was evident that the teacher had in mind the first—factories generally being UK-based and employing the English working class—but a boy pointed out that there were sugarcane factories on some islands. The exchange reinforced the idea that history was not simply about the recall of facts, but about how the use those facts as evidence in an argument can justify a historical interpretation (Entwistle, 2005). It also connoted that the classroom was a community of learners in which all voices, not just that of the teacher, were valued, a view emphasized in the last phase of this section of the lesson. A student, rather than David, described an overhead slide depicting the slave triangle to recap on what occurred at each the stage.

Deepening Understanding Through Student Dialogue

In the second and main activity of the lesson, the students were first given five, and later four more, contemporaneous pictures that illustrated aspects of the slave trade. Again, David explained that studying these pictures would deepen the students' understanding. The students worked on these in pairs. The dialogue between the two girls below is again suggestive of the way the

activity enabled students to think about both the historical content and processes for themselves and to develop their ideas by doing so:

> *Student 1:* Shall we put them in the triangle? [Pause—looking at
>   pictures.] That's when they're captured.
> *Student 2:* They're all wearing very nice clothes or ok clothes in this
>   picture. Do you think that could have been in Africa?
> *Student 1:* Um.
> *Student 2:* Because the clothes there are very different aren't they?
> *Student 1:* Maybe that's after this one.
> *Student 2:* Think that one.
> *Student 1:* So that goes like that.
> *Student 2:* But they're working there in the plantations.
> *Student 1:* Yeh. So maybe it's like that [moving pictures around]. I
>   think that's just before they get on this boat and this is when
>   they're captured and that could go there.
> *Student 2:* Mmm. What do you think this is?

In order to engage with the task, the students needed both to build on
the knowledge they had gained on the slave trade (which had been explored
in the first activity and the previous lesson) and to attend to the detail of the
pictures to give them evidence to sequence.

This need for synergy of activity was particularly clear in one of the
pictures and, significantly, it was on this picture that David focused as he
went around listening to the students and then used this in the whole-class
feedback on the activity. In this way, his actions were formative because he
used the evidence of the way the students had engaged with a task to further
the understanding of the whole class. The picture showed two groups of
Africans, one with guns, the other with spears. Most students had placed
this picture at the beginning of their sequence, seeing it as evidence of the
part that certain tribes played in the slave trade. The teacher's prompting
through questions, however, led the students to see that in order for the
Africans to have guns, they must already have traded, so another picture had
to come before this one. Significantly, however, at no point did David dic-
tate which picture this should be, and the students proffered at least two
suggestions, both of which were accepted.

The delicate balance between openness of decision making ("it's how
you justify it"; "there's a lot in what you say"; "there isn't a right answer")
and the improbability of certain choices in the sequencing of the pictures (as
in the picture with guns) began to induct students into the significance of
causal reasoning within history and the limits that source evidence places on
interpretation. In this way, the activity apprenticed students into the "guild

knowledge" necessary to progress within the discipline in a similar way to that of Angela's lesson. The nature of the dialogue, oral feedback, and questioning, both between peers and between the students and teacher, all contributed to this broad horizon. The particular content of the lesson contributed toward the more general historical aim.

Developing and Consolidating the Quality of Response

The final activity of the lesson both reinforced what had been achieved already and developed it further. Students were asked to write captions underneath each of the pictures. As with the English lessons, the teacher modeled the type of writing required before the students embarked on the task. Taking what was arguably the first picture of the sequence, David asked for contributions. Again, as in Angela's lesson, he developed and refined these. He began:

> *Teacher:* Why would you not write "Slaves walking across a field"?
> *Student:* Because they could be anywhere.
> *Teacher:* So?
> *Student:* Captured Africans taken to a ship.
> *Teacher:* Can we see a ship? How else could we add to it?
> *Student:* Captured Africans being marched to a ship on the West African coast.
> *Teacher:* Have we left anything else out?
> *Student:* Fellow African tribes capturing and taking their own people to captivity.

What is interesting about this exchange was the way that the teacher used questioning to push the student to develop the density and precision of the caption. As Angela and the classroom assistant had done with their performance, David set up an initial response, such as a student might make, to be critiqued and developed. Through the model, he made the criteria for a good caption clear. This was done less in terms of what was right and wrong than in terms of what would make for quality in a caption—in this case, evidential and inferential density about the slave trade from a visual source. In this way, subject content and processes were blended in the articulation of a caption. Moreover, the use of a caption is, in itself, a stepping-stone to enable students to use this type of language or discourse within an essay.

David then developed students' language or discourse capacity as he went around the class listening to and reading their attempts, again selecting one caption and exchange as a result of his sampling of student engagement. Moreover, in doing so, he added another dimension, one that might be called a moral dimension, to the exercise. As he went around the room, he had found two girls who had written a caption for one picture that said, "Slaves being sold at auction."

Teacher: How can you tell they are being auctioned?
Student: Because there's a sign that says "Horses, negroes, cattle."
Teacher: What's so bizarre and shocking about how that's set up?
Student: They're being sold as if they are cattle.

In the whole-class feedback, using the same two girls, David rehearsed this exchange for the rest of the students, having focused their attention on the relevant picture.

Teacher: What does that sign tell you?
Student: That they think of people in the same way as they do cows and horses.
Teacher: What else might you add to the caption, "Slaves sold at auction"?
Student: Slaves who are sold at auction are treated like items, not people.

The teacher used the girls as experts to enable the rest of the class to develop their own understanding. In this way, although he was orchestrating the commentary, he reinforced the sense that the classroom was a community where everyone learned from one another by focusing attention on the girls' observations.

The lesson ended with both a pointer to what was to come next and a reinforcement of what had been learned in the lesson so far—what can be learned from visual sources and their limitations.

Teacher: What other evidence would we need to have to understand the slave trade other than these pictures?
Student 1: Written documents.
Teacher: What kind of written documents?
Student 2: First-hand accounts of someone who is a slave.
Student 3: Or a slave owner. Get different points of view.
Teacher: What other kinds of things would you need to know about the triangle?
Student 4: Facts and figures of the numbers of people involved.

This last exchange demonstrates the students' existing knowledge of the importance of primary sources in building historical evidence, and gives them a clear indication of how this will be used in extending their understanding of the topic in which they are currently engaged.

CONCLUSIONS

This chapter has concentrated on the day-to-day business of the classroom rather than on written feedback on assignments. Mainly, this is because the efficacy of any written comments will largely depend on the extent to which the tasks have been set up and understood by the students, and this happens during the lessons. But it is also because this is where most formative assessment takes place—in the cut and thrust of the exchanges between student and student and teacher and student and the relationships this creates. It is during lessons that teachers have the most opportunity to engage with their students and help them progress by developing their thinking and their ability to articulate this within the subject discipline.

Teachers in English, the humanities, and social sciences use procedures such as questioning and feedback to develop and extend students' thinking in much broader terms than in, for example, math and science. (In these subjects, questioning and feedback are used almost diagnostically—first to identify and then to close a very specific gap in knowledge or conceptual understanding.) The interventions of English, humanities, and social science teachers are, moreover, often impromptu, arising directly out of the students' contributions, much in the way that ordinary, non-classroom dialogue takes place. The effectiveness of these interventions in developing thinking is entirely dependent on the richness of the tasks and the way they link together as the lesson progresses.

Similarly, sharing the criteria with the learner and peer and self-assessment need approaches and tasks that apprentice students into a "guild knowledge." This is more complex than a set of narrowly defined goals and can be better understood as a horizon toward which the students are taking varied paths, which the teacher helps them negotiate. In this way, AfL demands "high organization based on ideas" if it is going to help students become independent learners, because the nature of the tasks affects all subsequent interactions within the class.

The three lessons we have analyzed, while focusing on English and history, are illustrative of the way in which formative assessment is far more than a set of procedures. What we have called the "spirit of AfL" is operationalized in the way English, humanities, and social science teachers conceptualize and sequence the tasks undertaken by students in lessons. If the scope of the tasks is defined too narrowly, opportunities are missed.

If Dewey gives us an overarching principle for understanding what we are aiming for in AfL, Perrenoud's (1998) concept of the regulation of learning provides a helpful way of comprehending the dynamic of the classroom. For Perrenoud, formative assessment is really about the way teachers regulate learning. He describes different types of classrooms. In some of these classrooms, learning is highly regulated and prescribed. The scope of the activities is tightly defined. The outcomes of the learning are largely content-driven and predetermined, and students complete a series of narrow activities that are designed to cover the prescribed learning objectives. There is little opportunity for the students to own their own learning, and the only information it gives the teacher is a deficit model of what students cannot do according to the narrowly defined terms of reference.

In another type of classroom, the tasks are more open-ended, and thus, the scope for students to govern their own thinking is greater and the possibility for teachers to provide meaningful feedback is enhanced. In this type of classroom, "regulation does not include setting up activities suggested to, or imposed on the students but their adjustment once they have been initiated" (Perrenoud, 1998, p. 88). Angela's and David's lessons are examples of the latter, while Tracy's is an example of the former. Only when we understand the difference between these types of lessons, between the spirit and the letter of AfL and why they are so different, can we be effective formative teachers.

REFERENCES

Black, P., McCormick, R., James, M., & Pedder, D. (2006). Learning how to learn and assessment for learning: A theoretical inquiry. *Research Papers in Education, 21*(2), 119–132.

Black, P. J., & Wiliam, D. (1998). *Inside the black box: Raising standards through classroom assessment.* London: NFER, Nelson.

Bruner, J. S. (1963). *The process of education.* New York: Random House.

Dewey, J. (1966). *Experience and education.* London: Collier Books.

Entwistle, N. (2005). Learning outcomes and ways of thinking across contrasting disciplines and settings in higher education. *The Curriculum Journal, 16*(1), 67–82.

Hayden, T. (2004). History. In J. White (Ed.), *Rethinking the school curriculum: Values, aims and purposes.* London: Routledge Falmer.

Lambert, D. (2004). Geography. In J. White (Ed.), *Rethinking the school curriculum: Values, aims and purposes.* London: Routledge Falmer.

Marshall, B. (2000). *English teachers—the unofficial guide: Researching the philosophies of English teachers.* London: Routledge Falmer.

Marshall, B. (2004a). English. In J. White (Ed.), *Rethinking the school curriculum: Values, aims and purposes* (pp. 58–74). London: Routledge Falmer.

Marshall, B. (2004b). Goals or horizons—the conundrum of progression in English or a possible way of understanding formative assessment in English. *The Curriculum Journal, 15*, 101–113.

Marshall, B. (2004c). *English assessed: Formative assessment in English.* Sheffield, England: National Association of Teachers of English.

Marshall, B. (2006). *English inside the black box.* London: NFER Nelson.

Marshall, B., & Drummond, J. (2006). How teachers engage with formative assessment: Lessons from the classroom. *Research Papers in Education, 21*(2), 133–150.

Perrenoud, P. (1998). From formative evaluation to a controlled regulation of learning processes: Towards a wider conceptual field. *Assessment in Education: Principles, Policy and Practice, 5*(1), 85–102.

Sadler, R. (1989). Formative assessment and the design of instructional systems. *Instructional Science, 18*, 119–144.

Vygotsky, L. S. (1978). *Mind in society: The development of higher psychological processes.* Cambridge, MA: Harvard University Press.

Weelden, P., & Lambert, D. (2006). Geography inside the black box. London: NFER Nelson.

Wiliam, D. (2000). The meanings and consequences of educational assessments. *Critical Quarterly, 42*(1), 105–127.

About the Editor and Contributors

Lisa M. Abrams is assistant professor of education, Virginia Commonwealth University. She has authored journal articles and book chapters exploring the impact of high-stakes testing policies on teachers, students, and classroom practice. Her areas of expertise include classroom assessment, test-based accountability, high-stakes testing, graduation rates, and the implications of federal accountability policies for special education. A former classroom teacher, she received her Ph.D. in educational research, measurement, and evaluation from Boston College.

Susan M. Brookhart is an independent consultant. Her research interest is classroom assessment. Her articles have appeared in *Applied Measurement in Education, Teachers College Record, Journal of Educational Measurement*, and others. She is the 2007–2009 editor of *Educational Measurement: Issues and Practice*. Recent publications for practitioners include *Grading: Formative Assessment Strategies for Every Classroom* (2004) and *Educational Assessment of Students* (2007, with Anthony J. Nitko).

Gregory J. Cizek is professor of educational measurement and evaluation at the University of North Carolina at Chapel Hill, where he teaches courses in applied psychometrics, statistics, and research methods. His specializations include standard setting, testing security, and classroom assessment. He has managed national licensing and certification programs, worked on statewide student testing programs, served as an elected member of a local school board, and taught for five years as an elementary school teacher. His books include *Setting Performance Standards* (2001), *Cheating on Tests: How to Do It, Detect It, and Prevent It* (1999), and *Addressing Test Anxiety in a High-stakes Environment* (2006). He received his Ph.D. in measurement, evaluation, and research design from Michigan State University.

Thomas R. Guskey is professor of educational policy studies and evaluation at the University of Kentucky. His research interests focus on education reform, professional development, student assessment and grading practices, and mastery learning. He served on the Policy Research Team of the National Commission on Teaching & America's Future, on the Task Force to develop the National Standards for Staff Development, and recently was honored by the American Educational Research Association for his work relating research to practice. His most recent books include *Benjamin S. Bloom: Portraits of an Educator* (2005); *How's My Kid Doing? A Parents' Guide to Grades, Marks, and Report Cards* (2002); *Developing Grading and Reporting Systems for Student Learning* (2001); and *Implementing Mastery Learning* (1997).

Wynne Harlen has held several high-ranking positions, including Sidney Jones Professor of Science Education, head of the education department at the University of Liverpool, and director of the Scottish Council for Research in Education. She now works as a consultant in Scotland and has an honorary position as visiting professor at the University of Bristol. Her publications include 25 research reports, over 160 journal articles, 26 books of which she is sole or joint author, and contributions to 35 books on science education and assessment issues.

Siobhan Leahy is principal of Edmonton County School, a large secondary school in Greater London. After teaching mathematics in urban schools in London for 15 years, she served as the principal of two secondary schools for 12 years before moving to the United States. At the Educational Testing Service, she managed research on formative assessment and product development.

Bethan Marshall worked as an English teacher in London for 9 years before taking up her post at King's College there. Currently a senior lecturer in education, she specializes in issues relating to the teaching of English and assessment. She was part of the King's Medway Formative Assessment Project team and for 2 years the director of King's Learning How to Learn project. She has written extensively on the subject of English and assessment, including her book *English Teachers: An Unofficial Guide* (2000), and as a coauthor of *Assessment for Learning: Putting It into Practice* (2003).

James H. McMillan is professor of education at Virginia Commonwealth University and director of the Metropolitan Educational Research Consortium. His writing and research include books and articles in research methods, assessment, and educational psychology. Recently he has published *Classroom Assessment: Principles and Practice for Standards-Based Teaching* (2007) and *Assessment Essentials for Standards-Based Education* (in press). His research is in classroom assessment, student motivation, and student achievement.

Richard J. Stiggins is founder and executive director of the Educational Testing Service (ETS) Assessment Training Institute in Portland, Oregon. For nearly two decades, Rick and his team have provided the professional development teachers and school leaders need to design and implement quality assessment systems in their classrooms. For details, see www.ets.org/ati.

Dylan Wiliam is deputy director of the Institute of Education, University of London. After teaching mathematics and science in urban schools in London, he joined the faculty of King's College London, where he served as dean and assistant principal of the School of Education. From 2003 to 2006, he was senior research director at Educational Testing Service, Princeton, N.J. His main research interests center around the use of formative assessment as a focus for teacher professional development.

Index

NAMES

SUBJECTS